Praise for Mark Leslie Lefebvre

Mark was a critical hire at a critical time for Kobo. We knew independent publishing was a growing phenomenon in eBooks but needed the right person to create that all-important bridge with the author community. Mark performed that role perfectly, winning authors over to *Kobo Writing Life* with his combination of energy, lived experience as an author, genuine enthusiasm for how technology could extend a writer's reach. A truly valuable person.

—Michael Tamblyn, *CEO at Rakuten Kobo, Inc.*

Mark built KWL from the ground up, creating a self-publishing platform that is regarded as the best in the digital publishing industry, and a cornerstone of Kobo's content catalogue. He worked tirelessly to foster an authors-first philosophy he embodied at all times. He often traveled to conferences to present to crowds large and small to educate authors about Kobo and KWL. As a boss, Mark is a supportive mentor who is always available and supportive.

—Christine Munroe, *Director, KWL at Rakuten Kobo, Inc.*

Mark was a regular guest speaker for our students in the Creative Writing Program, at SFU Continuing Studies. His talks balanced providing encouraging information with the business realities of publishing. Our writers went away feeling excited about the publishing opportunities available to them, but also understood that though it is simple to publish through KWL or Amazon, success requires hard work. I personally enjoyed each one of Mark's presentations and would learn something new each time.

—Andrew Chesham, *Simon Fraser University*

Other Books in this Series

The 7 P's of Publishing Success

What seven traits do the most successful authors have in common? Which strategic approaches have the most positive effect? Where should you focus for maximum results?

Indie Publishing Insider Secrets

Insights, Wisdom and Stark Perspectives on Writing, Publishing, and Bookselling Success From a 25-Year Book Industry Representative.

Feb 2019

KILLING IT ON KOBO

Mark Leslie Lefebvre

STARK
PUBLISHING SOLUTIONS
Stark Publishing Solutions

Stark Publishing Solutions
An Imprint of Stark Publishing
Waterloo, Ontario
www.starkpublishing.ca

Publisher's Note: This work is derived from the author's experience in bookselling, writing and publishing and six years as the Director of Kobo Writing Life. It is meant to inform and inspire writers with tools and best practice strategies for success in publishing direct to Kobo. The author and publisher believe that there is no single magic solution for everyone and that advice, wisdom and insights should be carefully curated and adapted to suit each individual's needs, goals and desires.

Killing it on Kobo / Mark Leslie Lefebvre
October 2018

Print ISBN: 978-1-7751478-4-8
eBook ISBN: 978-1-7751478-5-5
Audio ISBN: 978-1-7751478-6-2

This one is for the authors who made and who continue to make Kobo Writing Life a huge success. Kobo built it, but it wasn't the fully-realized dream until the authors came, published, and conquered.

TABLE OF CONTENTS

PREFATORY DISCLAIMER

THIS BOOK is a summation of my experiences, beliefs, and practices as they relate to Kobo.

While it does draw upon my six years of experience as *Director of Self-Publishing and Author Relations* at Kobo, it is not meant to represent the viewpoint or perspective of Rakuten Kobo Inc. or any of its employees, past, present or future.

My aim is to leverage my expertise to help benefit authors and publishers looking to optimize their own engagement with this global retailer.

Great care was taken to ensure that the statistics shared in this book – and in my consulting work with authors and publishers – do not violate any confidentiality terms. Thus, the materials you are about to read are all items that have been previously shared publicly either by myself or other representatives from Kobo to publisher and author audiences over the years. These details are, subject to change based on market conditions and standard industry evolution.

They are meant to inform and inspire you with tools and best practice strategies. But I strongly believe there is no single "magic bullet" solution for everyone. The insights contained herein should be carefully adapted to suit your own individual needs and goals.

INTRODUCTION: Why This Book?

THIS WAS A book that not only needed to be written, but it's a book I was meant to write.

There are plenty of books containing tips, strategies and marketing techniques to optimize sales on Kindle. But there are very few books with a specific focus on Kobo.

As of this writing, Kobo is one of the five largest eBook commerce sites on the planet. When I left Kobo in November 2017, Kobo Writing Life was the biggest single source of weekly unit sales, representing 1 in every 4 books sold in English, and 1 in every 5 books sold in all languages on Kobo.

The list of authors who cite Kobo as their second-best platform for sales continues to grow each year; and there are a cohort of writers who claim Kobo is the retailer where they earn their highest source of revenue.

If you are interested in being one of the authors leveraging the global power of Kobo, then this book is for you.

I worked as *Director of Self-Publishing & Author Relations* at Kobo for six years. I was hired in the fall of 2011 and tasked with coming up with a solution for making it easier for self-published authors and small publishers to easily get their titles in to the Kobo catalog. I was the driving force behind the creation of Kobo Writing Life, the publish-direct to Kobo platform, and worked as that platform's champion both internally and externally, hiring staff that had an author-centric approach, and constantly soliciting feedback from the writing community to make the platform better.

After all, I was the very first author to sign up for *Kobo Writing Life.*

So, who better to write such a book?

I'll never forget that fateful morning when I was sitting down for an early morning meeting with Michael Tamblyn, current CEO of Rakuten Kobo Inc, at a restaurant in Toronto, Ontario to discuss the opportunity. But prior to getting to that significant moment in my career as a bookseller, I must take a slight digression to explain how that breakfast meeting took place. It is a bit of a tangential path, but I'm a strong believer in the importance of context.

If you just want to get to the heart of the learnings, then you may want to skip the backstory of the chapter entitled ***My Path to Kobo*** and move right on to ***Kobo 101***.

And if you are already intimately familiar with Kobo and are using this book to "up" your game at Kobo, then you may even want to skip further ahead to where the advanced information starts from ***Optimizing Pre-Order Sales*** and the chapters beyond.

If, however, you are hungry for a taste of the background and the road that led me to Kobo, there's a spot at the table for you to sit down beside Michael and me as well as an empty mug in front of you ready to be filled with that rich, hot, and delicious blend of fresh roasted coffee.

So, whether you read the full menu top to bottom or jump right to the menu item that appeals to you the most, let's dig in and get this meal started.

MY PATH TO KOBO

IN THE SUMMER of 2011 Kobo's Michael Tamblyn and I sat down for a breakfast in the West-Toronto Liberty Village restaurant *School* located on a street kitty-corner from Kobo's head office.

At the time, Tamblyn was the *Executive Vice President of Content, Sales & Merchandising* for Kobo, an independent upstart company that had been founded and was majority owned by Indigo Books and Music, Inc, Canada's largest and single dominant book chain. Michael Serbinis was the company's CEO at the time.

I knew both Michaels from previous work experience.

Michael Serbinis had been Indigo's CTO (Chief Technical Officer) when I was working on the IT team as *Database Quality Manager* about five years previously. And MT (the name Michael Tamblyn was internally christened with so that people didn't confuse which Kobo senior executive was being referred to) had been President of BookNet Canada when I was on the original metadata committee and then, later, a board member.

I had been working at the bookstore at McMaster University as *Book Operations Manager*, overseeing the Trade Book, Text Book, and Custom Courseware teams and had already been dabbling in eBook publishing. In 2008 I purchased an Espresso Book Machine for the bookstore and McMaster became the 2nd location in Canada and the 9th in the world to own one.

For those who aren't familiar with an Espresso Book Machine (EBM) it is a print on demand (POD) machine from On Demand Books, LLC. The EBM is designed to sit at the point of sale (typically in a bookstore or library) and to print, collate, and bind a trade paperback quality book right on the spot in a matter of minutes from a digital file. On Demand Books, based in New York City, was founded by Jason Epstein (Chairman), Dane Neller (CEO) and Thor Sigvaldason (CTO).

Since 1999, Epstein had been envisioning a line of "next-generation" POD technology machines that would be fully automatic and could be placed in neighborhood bookshops, coffee shops, newsstands, or even in hotel lobbies, airport terminals and on cruise ships. A prototype of the machine, filed for patent in 1993 and granted in 2001, was created by St. Louis engineer and inventor Jeff Marsh. On Demand Books, founded in 2003, worked at developing Marsh's machine and integrating it with a digital catalog. The first beta machine was installed at the

World Bank in Washington, D.C. in April 2006. In September of that year, the second beta machine was installed at The Library of Alexandria in Egypt.

The technology and concept behind On Demand Books and the Espresso Book Machine was, prior to the advent of eBooks, the single biggest revolution to hit publishing since, perhaps, the advent of the mass market paperback. The vision involved replacing the centralized supply chain for the distribution of physical books in a radically de-centralized and direct-to-consumer model. It was a tried, tested and true "publish globally, print locally" model. With the *EspressNet* digital catalog of more than seven million licensed in-copyright and public domain works it meant consumers could walk into a bookstore, browse from a virtual catalog of millions of titles, and then wait approximately five to fifteen minutes for the book to be downloaded, printed and bound right on the spot.

Essentially, a book could be delivered direct to a bookstore in the time it might take to order and prepare an espresso at a neighborhood coffee shop.

Because Titles Bookstore at McMaster University was owned by the department of Student Affairs and followed a strong student-first mandate, with revenues used to fund and support the University's Student Union operations, we had always been looking at ways to save students money. The Custom Courseware business, originally designed to do that, ran into cost related issues that were a combination of exorbitant fees from Access Copyright, Canada's national licensing organization for the remixing, copying and distribution of content for educational and professional purposes, as well as internal political snafus where unionization led to inefficiencies in terms of process, time and cost. The structure behind these "custom coursepacks" ended up costing as much, if not more, than the over-priced textbooks themselves, leaving students with what they felt was an inferior and over-priced "photocopied" product.

The other alternative to saving students money was Used Textbooks. But the challenge in that business was the struggle of the 3-year-cycle of new editions forced onto academia by the publishers; not to mention that neither publishers nor authors receive any royalties for the sale and exchange of these products. While I was all for saving students money, I also respected the need for content creators to be paid for their work. Or, more accurately, be paid a reasonable price for their work.

My idea behind the purchase of an EBM was to source textbooks directly from publishers and content creators and, with the issue of "returns" and "shipping" removed, significantly reduce the distribution costs. Those savings would be passed directly on to the students.

In the first two years of the machine's operation this resulted in saving McMaster students millions of dollars. Achievement unlocked!

But, one of the side-effects of having a machine that can print and bind a book in a matter of minutes right on the spot is how it attracts local writers. Between the seasonal printing of textbooks, the machine was used to help local self-published authors realize their dreams of seeing their work in print without having to either purchase thousands of copies (the ideal print-run on an EBM is one copy) or without having to fall prey to the dozens of vulture-style online POD-related "Vanity Press" companies that had been partially responsible for giving self-publishing a bad name.

Creating a local self-publishing POD business with integrity and the desire to help authors rather than prey on their hopes and dreams and trick them out of thousands of dollars (like so many "Vanity Press" operations), was, in effect, a virtual licence to print money.

That operation at McMaster was a huge success. And it was happening at the time the eBook revolution was just beginning.

In 2006 Sony's release of the PSR-500 was a dramatic step forward in eBook reading consumption. And when the Kindle was launched in 2007, that began to completely revolutionize the book industry and make way for an entirely new option for self-published authors.

Kobo, originally launched under the name Shortcovers in 2009, (one year after I had acquired the Espresso Book Machine) was Canada's answer to the Kindle.

Not long into my EBM experience, I realized I'd been printing and shipping POD books from Hamilton, Ontario to locations around the world. At the time there were still perhaps only a dozen EBMs around the world, and the integration with Ingram's Lightning Source Inc. (a POD subsidiary of the Ingram Book Group, which powers Ingram Spark along with POD solutions for the world's largest publishers) was still in its infancy.

I was looking to leverage digital in a way that my locally published books, via the "Titles on Demand" imprint could allow more comprehensive digital distribution without requiring a sophisticated and expensive local POD operation like an EBM.

So, I created an account with Amazon via their KDP (Kindle Direct Publishing) platform for global distribution. Toronto-based Kobo (about an hour's drive from McMaster), didn't have a similar portal, but did have a publishing program that relied on FTP transfer of files and metadata submitted electronically. Because I had been behind the original creation of the human-friendly "Excel template" for transmission of metadata and had already managed the import of publisher data to a digital catalog when I had worked at Chapters Online and Indigo Books and Music, it was easy enough for me to also use this type of system to publish the books direct to Kobo.

I had been at the bookstore at McMaster University for about five years, and, while the experience had been amazing, I was getting frustrated with a significant shift in the culture and climate. The bookstore was migrating away from books (from actually being a bookstore) and became more focused on the selling of McMaster branded clothing, other swag and gift or chachkies (derived from "tchotchke" a Slavic term for "trinket" or the Yiddish "tshotshke"). I was all about the books and was slowly becoming de-motivated with the new vision and focus for the store.

With my interest in how digital publishing opportunities could re-invigorate the book and publishing industry, and with my ongoing championing of POD and digital technologies via the EBM, my mind had been opened to new possibilities.

Which is what led to sitting down with Michael Tamblyn for breakfast that fateful morning in the summer of 2011.

"We believe that eBook self-publishing will not only open up new opportunities for writers," Michael said in the heart of a lively and energetic conversation where we had barely glanced at the menu, "but that it will allow for the discovery of great talent, and, ultimately, lead to growth in publishing itself."

I know that we ate a full breakfast and drank plenty of coffee that morning, but, for the life of me, I can't remember the meal; though I know, from years of eating there, *School* makes a most excellent breakfast. But I do remember the mutual thrill and excitement that energized the table and the air around us.

Though Michael and I had known one another for years, that breakfast had felt, in many ways, like a first date where the two parties completely hit it off. We were finishing each others' sentences, enthusiastically coming up with creative ideas on the spot.

While I would like to believe I had made some intelligent and forward-thinking visionary statements during that breakfast, I imagine I may have just been sitting there nodding my head vigorously like an idiot as Michael described a role he had been championing to create at Kobo.

He was describing a person who not only understood the publishing and bookselling landscape, but also was intimately familiar with and sympathetic to the author's perspective. He outlined a visionary who could merge the understanding of the business and margins of bookselling and publishing into a successful operation that paid strong attention to the needs of the creators who would not only want to be a part of this movement, but, would, in ways, prefer to have such a solution available to them.

Michael knew I had been a bookseller since 1992. He knew I had self-published my first book using POD in 2004. He also knew that I not only embraced self-publishing but that I did it without dis-respecting the value that traditional publishing brought to our industry.

He knew I had been behind the creation of a portal for small publishers to upload their content to Indigo Books and Music. He knew, via my experience working with BookNet Canada, my admiration for the sharing of data and that I was a stickler for the quality of book metadata.

He knew of my successes leveraging digital POD technology at McMaster University. He knew my student-first approach at McMaster would be akin to my author-first mentality, and that I would always seek to find the best compromise between generosity to the creator and a savvy business bottom line.

He, perhaps, also knew that I could find ways to push the envelope, or perhaps even break the rules or create new rules because of my understanding of and respect for the existing laws and rules surrounding publishing and bookselling.

I think, perhaps, the one intelligent thing I might have said that morning was the following, which came towards the end of that breakfast.

"Michael," I said over-top of the coffee cup perched in my tented-arms in the sip-ready position. "This person, this role, this vision you have described is me. The only thing missing in all of this is the most obvious name that should be attached to it. Mine."

A few months later, in the newly christened role of *Director of Self-Publishing and Author Relations* I was welcomed to the Kobo office, given a desk, a laptop, a phone and given the task of coming up with a plan for self-publishing success at Kobo.

The people at Kobo are among the most intelligent, passionate and innovative people I have ever had the pleasure of working with. From the very first day to my very last, I felt honored to be among my kind of people, with the underlying focus of bringing writer and reader together in the passion for reading always being at the heart of every decision.

I spearheaded the creation of Kobo Writing Life, the direct-to-Kobo publishing platform, which was launched in the summer of 2012. By the time I left Kobo in November of 2017, a little more than six years after I had started there, I was not only proud of what we had built from the ground-up, but that Kobo Writing Life was the largest single publishing source in terms of weekly unit sales at

Kobo. Or, in other terms, selling more units per week than the world's largest publishers.

I am proud of the work that I have done as a part of that, but even more proud of all the people at Kobo who supported that vision and the current Kobo Writing Life team and the authors who publish their books to Kobo who continue to realize their writing and publishing dreams every single day.

So, now that we have a bit of the backstory out of the way, let's call for the check, start gathering our things, and then head across the street to take a peek at the Kobo offices and I'll start off with giving you the basic virtual tour of the place.

KOBO 101

LET'S START WITH a basic understanding of what Kobo is.

Some of the information in this chapter you might already be familiar with. But I'm willing to bet there are at least a half dozen tidbits the average writer never knew about Kobo. After 6 years of sharing knowledge via media, interviews, podcasts, blogs and during thousands of conversations, I realized that very little of the information being relayed was actually retained by authors.

So, I put this together to provide that information in a handy and accessible format.

What is Kobo?

Kobo was born in Canada out of the country's largest

book retailer, Indigo Books & Music — similar to Barnes & Noble in the US or WHSmith in the UK. Originally launched in December 2009 as *Shortcovers,* a cloud-based e-reading service, the concept behind the company, and the vision of Michael Serbinis, the founder, was that any-one should be able to read any book on any device at any time.

By December 2009, the company was spun-off from Indigo into an independent company under the name Kobo, with Indigo as the majority owner and with global investors that included Borders, Cheung Kong Holdings and REDgroup Retail. The www.kobo.com website and bookstore was launched with localization to 16 different countries and with a catalog of millions of titles in their eBook catalog.

In January of 2012, Kobo was acquired by and is a sub-sidiary of Rakuten, a Japanese digital company with an Amazon-sized presence in Asia and other global territo-ries. While most people in the United States who are fa-miliar with Kindle and have, perhaps, never heard of Kobo (or, officially, Rakuten Kobo, Inc.), the company's ownership by Rakuten, Inc. (Japan's largest e-commerce site) whose sister companies include PriceMinister, Play.com, Wuaki.tv, Viber, Ebates, Viki, Slice, LinkShare, and OverDrive gives it an incredibly powerful global presence.

Kobo not only has free apps available on tablets, smartphones and desktop computers, but it also manu-factures a line of award-winning eReader devices that use an electronic ink screen. The readers, which, in the summer of 2018 included the Kobo Aura ONE, the Kobo Aura H_2O Edition 2, the Kobo Clara HD, the Kobo Aura Edition 2, and the Kobo Forma support the industry ePub standard for reading, and also have multiple waterproof design features. *Digital Trends* described the Kobo Aura One as their top eBook reader to buy in a summer of 2018 article, and many of their devices have been cited by places such as *PCMag, Forbes, Business Insider, Wired* and *CNET* as among the top eReaders in the world.

Because of the company's connection to Japan, many assume that the name "Kobo" is of Japanese origin. The reality is that Kobo is an anagram of the word "book." That is, perhaps, a little piece of trivia you might be able to use during a friendly bar-bet to secure yourself a free drink or appetizer.

Why Kobo?

While many authors see the largest percentage of their sales via Amazon Kindle –Amazon is, after all, the world's largest online bookstore – those same authors (if they bother to look) will likely also find that the majority of those sales originate in the US and the UK.

Because Kobo and other eBook retail platforms like Apple Books (formerly iBooks), spent a significant amount of time in the earlier days of the eBook boom focusing on markets outside the US, the sales aren't concentrated in America.

Kobo's EVP of Business Development, Todd Humphrey was quoted in a September 27, 2013 *Forbes* article by Ava Seave entitled "Digital Reading Company Kobo 'On Pace To Be A Billion Dollar Company," as saying: "From day 1, we made it our goal and a priority to be international." Humphrey went on to say that if they weren't international, they wouldn't be able to get to scale.

In a January 2012 *Wired* article, the magazine cited Kobo as "the only global competitor to Amazon" in the eBook market. Rakuten CEO Hiroshi Mikitani has publicly stated that Kobo is number one in France, ahead of Amazon in Japan as well as in Australia and New Zealand. Partnerships in the Netherlands, in Italy and in other European companies had led to Kobo having a far stronger presence there, as well. Also, because of the company's Canadian origins, it has a far stronger market foot-hold and brand recognition within Canada.

If you are content to sell in the US, and perhaps in the UK, then Amazon is likely still your best bet for the majority of your sales and income. Of course, as of the writing of this, Kobo just launched a US-based partnership with Walmart, powering the Walmart eBooks brand (Walmart eBooks by Rakuten Kobo). This service – intended to bring eBooks to Walmart customers both online and in-store – represents Walmart's continued fight with Amazon, and could mean a growth for Kobo eBook sales in the United States.

However, if you are looking to expand your sales to other countries and to gain a readership in other global territories, and, perhaps most importantly, not be dependent upon a single retailer for the majority of your writing income (also known as "publishing wide"), leveraging Kobo should be among the strategies that you employ.

Ways that Kobo Differs from Amazon

Kobo is Only About Books and About Reading

Unlike Amazon, whose entire service is centred around selling any and all products, Kobo is entirely focused on the experience of readers via eBooks and audiobooks. They also take a human approach to merchandising — that is, deciding which books to promote, and to whom. This is similar to how good physical bookstores work, as opposed to Amazon, who allow their algorithm to make most of the merchandising decisions. It also has an effect on pricing strategies, since books aren't part of a "loss leader" strategy to sell other products — they're the only thing that Kobo sells.

The Rakuten Advantage

Because Rakuten owns several complimentary digital companies, authors can leverage that to expand their reach and market presence. For example, OverDrive will help you get your books into local library systems, while LinkShare will let you create affiliate links that will help get other people promoting and selling your book.

Kobo Partners with Retailers Across the World

Kobo partners with dozens of global physical and online retailers around the world such as WHSmith (UK), Mondadori (Italy), FNAC (France), BOL (Netherlands) and American Booksellers Association and Walmart in the US. When you publish to Kobo, your book also appears in the catalogs of thousands of these global partners. Instead of competing, Kobo collaborates with those retailers. Unlike Amazon, with an operation meant to compete with and dominate the market, Kobo seeks out collaborative bookselling operations, leveraging their strengths in digital, eBook and audiobook sales with their partner's strengths in selling physical books.

This collaborative approach is quite Canadian, eh?

A Look at Kobo's Global Retail Partners

As of the summer of 2018, the webstores powered by Kobo include:

- American Booksellers Association (variety of participant websites) www.indiebound.org/ebooks
- Angus & Robertson/BookWorld (Australia/formerly Borders AU) www.angusrobertson.com.au
- Bol (Netherlands) www.bol.com
- Collins (Australia) www.collinsbooks.com.au
- Feltrinelli (Italy) www.lafeltrinelli.it
- FNAC (France) www.fnac.com
- FNAC (Portugal) www.fnac.pt

- Gandhi (Mexico) www.gandhi.com.mx
- Indigo (Canada) www.chapters.indigo.ca
- La Central (Spain) www.lacentral.com
- Livraria Cultura (Brazil) www.livrariacultura.com.br
- Mondadori (Italy) www.librimondadori.it
- National Book Store (Philippines) http://www.nationalbookstore.com.ph/ *
- PaperPlus (New Zealand) www.paperplus.co.nz
- PriceMinister (France) www.priceminister.com
- Librería Porrúa (Mexico) www.porrua.mx
- Rakuten (Japan) www.global.rakuten.com/en/
- Walmart (US) www.walmart.com/cp/5632020
- WHSmith (Great Britain) www.whsmith.co.uk

* This URL won't work for people outside the local territory. It will re-direct.

Kobo Writing Life's Royalty Structure is Far More Generous Than KDP's

Kobo Writing Life authors and publishers receive a 70% or 45% royalty rate on each eBook sold through the Kobo store. eBooks that are priced according to the following pricing rules are eligible to receive a 70% royalty rate:

- CAD – Canadian Dollar – greater than or equal to $2.99
- AUD – Australian Dollar – greater than or equal to $2.99

- GBP – British Pound Sterling – greater than or equal to £1.99
- EUR – Euro – greater than or equal to €1.99
- NZD – New Zealand Dollar – greater than or equal to $2.99
- HKD – Hong Kong Dollar – greater than or equal to $15.99
- JPY – Japanese Yen – greater than or equal to ¥299
- CHF – Swiss Franc – greater than or equal to 2.99
- TRY – Turkish Lira – greater than or equal to ₺5.99
- BRL – Brazilian Real – greater than or equal to R$7.99
- MXN – Mexican Peso – greater than or equal to $39.99
- TWD – Taiwan Dollar – greater than or equal to $70
- ZAR – South African Rand – greater than or equal to R29.99
- PHP – Philippine Peso – greater than or equal to ₱99.99
- INR – Indian Rupee – greater than or equal to ₹149.99

If your book is priced under any of these values, a sale in that territory/currency will result in a royalty of 45% instead of 70%. There are four things about this that are unique and set Kobo Writing Life apart in a positive way.

1st, Kindle Direct Publishing (KDP) uses a range with a "below" and "above" cut-off for 70%. On KDP, if you price below $2.99 USD or above $9.99 you will not earn the full 70%. On Kobo there is a price "floor" but no price "ceiling." I talk about that in more detail in the chapter on price optimization, because this is a major positive when it comes to earning more at Kobo.

2nd, KDP has Delivery Costs that aren't obvious nor apparent. You actually aren't earning the full 70% via KDP even when you think you are. It is a tiny difference, but tiny differences all add up over time. Kindle has a somewhat hidden "file size" processing fee they charge for any file where you are earning 70%.

The following text is from Kindle's Digital Pricing Page, accessed in August 2018, and appears on this page (https://kdp.amazon.com/en_US/help/topic/G200634500) in the chart under **C. Delivery Costs**

Delivery Costs are equal to the number of megabytes we determine your Digital Book file contains, multiplied by the Delivery Cost rate listed below.

Amazon.com: US $0.15/MB
Amazon.ca: CAD $0.15/MB
Amazon.com.br: R$0.30/MB
Amazon.co.uk: UK £0.10/MB
Amazon.de: €0,12/MB
Amazon.fr: €0,12/MB
Amazon.es: €0,12/MB
Amazon.in: INR ₹7/MB
Amazon.it: €0,12/MB

Amazon.nl: €0,12/MB
Amazon.co.jp: ¥1/MB
Amazon.com.mx: MXN $1/MB
Amazon.com.au: AUD $0.15/MB

We will round file sizes up to the nearest kilobyte. The minimum Delivery Cost for a Digital Book will be US$0.01 for sales in US Dollars, INR₹1 for sales in Indian Rupees, CAD$0.01 for sales in CAD Dollars, £0.01 for sales in GB Pounds, ¥1 in JPY, R$0.01 for sales in Brazilian Reais, MXN$1 for sales in Mexican Pesos, AUD$0.01 for sales in Australian Dollars, and €0.01 for sales in Euros, regardless of file size. For sales in JPY, we will not deduct any Delivery Cost for books 10 MB or greater.

Thus, a book that sells for $4.99 USD and in which you are supposed to earn 70% ($3.49) will actually earn you one penny less at the very best, with the smallest possible file size ($3.48) or, more likely, a few pennies. KDP actually shows you this value, but many authors have never actually done the math.

Using a personal example, my book *Evasion*, which is priced at $4.99 USD, shows the following.

My book file is 0.4 MB, thus, instead of earning $3.49 per unit sale, I am earning $3.45. It is only 4 cents less per unit sale, but if I have sold 50,000 copies, that comes to $2,000 that has been shaved off and is not in my pocket. Those pennies add up.

This isn't news and isn't particularly shocking; but I am surprised that this rarely ever comes up when authors compare retailers. From a purely business perspective, based on the volume of sales that KDP sees, this likely lines Amazon's pockets will millions upon millions of dollars.

3rd, unlike Amazon's Kindle Direct Publishing, which requires that ALL of the territories abide by the price floor or price ceiling rule before you can earn 70% in ANY of them, you can have a book priced ABOVE the threshold in one country and BELOW the threshold in another, and Kobo will pay you the appropriate 70% or 45% accordingly. Amazon, however, will penalize all of your territory/currency sales.

For example, if you have a book on sale in the US only for $0.99 USD and it is priced $2.99 in CAD and AUD and £1.99 GBP and €1.99 EUR on Kobo, you would earn 0.45% for sales in USD and 70% for sales in CAD, AUD, GBP and EUR. However, on Kindle, you would earn 35% in all of USD, CAD, AUD, GBP and EUR.

The same would hold true if you manually set a price above $9.99 in a single territory. All the other territory earnings would drop to 35%.

4th, at the low end, KDP pays 35% and Kobo pays 45%. Again, this is only a 10% difference, but it is something that can add up over time. In an exercise I like to show authors when reminding them about the cost/investment and return on a book and the earnings vs unit sales of various price points, I typically use the following example.

Because the average cost of the various expenses that go into crafting and publishing an eBook can be anywhere from $300 to $3000 USD, here's how the breakdown would work for an author to earn back that investment.

Priced at $4.99 USD, the author would have to sell:

- 86 copies to earn back $300 (The number might more likely be 87 or 88 copies once you factor in the minimal delivery cost per unit sale at KDP)
- 857 copies to earn back $3000 (via KDP)
- 667 copies to earn back $3000 (via KWL)

However, priced at $0.99 USD, the author would have to sell:

- 857 copies to earn back $300 via KDP
- 667 copies to earn back $300 via KWL
- 8,571 copies to earn back $3000 via KDP
- 6,667 copies to earn back $3000 via KWL

Again, these are small value differences, but those differences add up over time and result in making a difference in the money that is in your pocket versus the money in the retailer's pocket.

Like that four cents in delivery costs or the ten percent difference on lower priced titles, many of the strategies in this book aren't about any single "magic bullet" solution, but about incremental and consistent increases over time.

Me, I'm always a fan of money in my pocket, and if incremental increases over time are the way that happens, I'm all for that.

How about you?

Now that we've taken a basic overview of Kobo itself, let's dig into the publish-direct option of Kobo Writing Life.

There are other ways to get your eBook to Kobo, but the focus for this book, however, will explore how you can use Kobo Writing Life to take full advantage of the benefits that come with publishing to Kobo.

And in the next chapter we'll navigate our way through KWL.

NAVIGATING THE BASICS OF KOBO WRITING LIFE

AS MENTIONED IN my backstory and lead in to Kobo, I was behind the creation of Kobo Writing Life, Kobo's direct-publishing platform, which was launched in the summer of 2012. So, as you can expect, I'm a bit partial to and biased towards using Kobo Writing Life when publishing to Kobo.

Yes, there are multiple ways to publish to Kobo's catalog, that include Smashwords, Draft2Digital, PublishDrive, StreetLib and many other places. And for some authors who are perhaps interested in using a single source of publishing their books to all retailers, using one of this distributors might make sense. You give up a bit of control, and a bit of margin when you use a third party to distribute to Kobo. But the gain is in simplicity and the time that you save. Each author needs to make their own decision on the costs of each.

Ten years ago, if an author asked for a recommendation on the best single source for publishing wide, I would have suggested Smashwords. But in the intervening years, the intuitive interface, dynamic functionality and global pricing controls at Draft2Digital have made this the preferred third-party distribution platform.

But if you want to leverage the best of all possible worlds for your global sales, at the time of the writing of this book, you are best off taking advantage of the focus and incredible investment that Kobo has placed in their self-publishing direct platform.

This chapter will include a high-level look at the basics of the Kobo Writing Life platform. Like I mentioned in the introduction, you might want to skip ahead. If you are already familiar with the basics, you may want to jump straight to the next chapter (***Optimizing Pre-Order Sales***) where the meat of the strategies begin. You can always later refer to this chapter as a quick an easy reference should one of those strategies mention a section of the KWL dashboard that you are not familiar with.

To use Kobo Writing Life you need to sign up for an author account. If you don't already have one, go to www.kobo.com/writinglife and sign up for a free KWL author account. Having an account is likely to help with visualization of some of the basics that I walk through for eBook publishing and other features of Kobo Writing Life.

For an up-to-date or more comprehensive look at these steps, check out the Kobo Writing Life Author Guide. There are links to it from inside the **Help** section of Kobo Writing Life as well as the Zendesk Kobo Writing Life online help centre at:

https://kobowritinglife.zendesk.com/hc/en-us

Creating a Kobo Writing Life Account

1) Go to www.kobo.com/writinglife
2) Click on the **Get Started** button
3) If you have a Kobo account (ie, a reader account), enter your email address and then your password and then click **Continue**
4) If you do not have a Kobo account, click on the **News? Sign up here** button
    a. Enter your email address
    b. Enter the password you wish to use
    c. Confirm the password you wish to use
    d. Choose your email language preference
    e. Review the *Terms of Use* and *Privacy Policy* (You need to **Accept** Kobo's terms in order to complete the creation of your account)
    f. Click **Continue**
    g. Enter your Contact Information
    h. Enter your First Name
    i. Enter your Last Name

j. Enter your Publisher Name (This field is optional. In my case, I have published my own titles under "Stark Publishing" since 2004, so I would enter that here)
k. Enter your email address
l. Select if you would like to receive email updates
m. Enter your telephone number (optional)
n. Enter an existing Kobo publishing account ID (optional, and if you haven't published to Kobo direct prior to July 2012, ignore this field. It was created to help link legacy accounts to new KWL accounts for payment purposes)
o. Enter your mailing address
p. Review the **Email Settings**
    i. *Kobo News and Updates* – general Kobo news, sales and promotions
    ii. *Kobo Writing Life News and Updates* – KWL specific news and the monthly newsletter
    iii. *When your Books are published* – a notification email when your new books are published
    iv. *When your updates to eBooks are live (beta)* – a notification that your updates to a previously published book are live in the store
q. Select **How you Discovered Us** to let Kobo know how you found out about Kobo

Writing Life (If this book is the reason, just ell them: "Mark Lefebvre's book sent me")

r. Click **Save and continue**

5) Review the *Terms of Service*
6) Click **Save and Next**
7) Verify your email address

Once you go through the steps above you will be required to set up your banking/payment information. Payments at Kobo are sent via Electronic Fund Transfer directly to your bank account.

You will not be able to publish a book to Kobo until you have entered your banking information. This is because they a) need to set up a default currency for your publishing and b) need to have a way to pay you before they can sell any of your books

The banking information is also one of many preventative "road-blocks" to help reduce fraudulent use of Kobo Writing Life.

To add in your banking details, click on the *My Account* dropdown in the upper right section of the upper header and the select *Payment Information*. In the *Bank Information* area, complete the following steps:

1) *Select your country* - Your currency information will, by default, be associated with whatever country you are in. If you are in Canada, it will default to CAD. If you are in the US, it will default to USD. If you are in a country where the default currency

isn't supported for payment, USD will be the default currency.

2) *Enter bank branch details* (SWIFT Code, Routing Code or IBAN associated with your bank) – this is, perhaps, the most complicated and confusing part of the process. See the handy publishing guides and FAQ in the Kobo Writing Life help center at www.kobowritinglife.zendesk.com for full details, support and help
3) *Select your bank branch*
4) *Enter your account details*
5) *Click* **Save Changes**

If you are unable to find your bank or enter your banking information, you are advised to contact the KWL team directly at writinglife@kobo.com for further help and support

Header Level Navigation

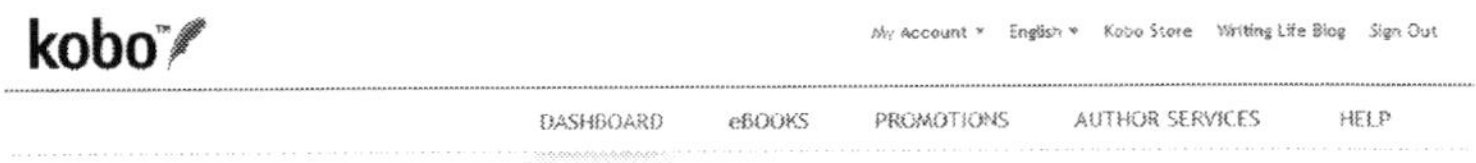

My Account

Various ways to manage your contact and payment information as well as review the Terms of Service

- **Payment Information:** *Enter or update your banking info for direct deposit. You can also see the history of the* *monthly invoices of what Kobo owes you and a history of payments made to your account.*

- **Contact Information:** *Enter or update your contact information as well as control the different notification emails from Kobo, Kobo Writing Life and metadata updates.*
    - *The first checkbox (Kobo news and updates) is useful to see and understand what types of promotional emails Kobo sends to their customers.*
    - *The second (Kobo Writing Life news and updates) ensures you receive the monthly KWL newsletter.*
    - *The last two checkboxes provide info on when a new book is published or when your price or other metadata updates have made it to the production catalog.*
- **Terms of Service:** *Review the KWL terms of service that you agreed to when setting up your account.*

Language

This is where you control the language that the KWL dashboard is presented in. The default is English. French, Italian, Spanish, German, Dutch and Japanese are available.

Kobo Store

A link to the Kobo webstore (www.kobo.com).

Writing Life Blog

A link to the Kobo Writing Life blog (www.kobowritinglife.com) for articles from the KWL team, spotlights on articles and other feature updates

Sign Out

Where you can log out of your account.

Main Navigation TABS on KWL

Below is a list of the main navigation TABS you will see below the top header of KWL when you log in to it.

- ***DASHBOARD***
    - ***SALES AT A GLANCE***
    - ***SALES BY BOOK***
    - ***SALES BY REGION***
- ***EBOOKS***
- ***PROMOTIONS***
- ***AUTHOR SERVICES***
- ***HELP***

DASHBOARD

On the Dashboard (which is where you land by default when you log in) you can monitor the sales of your book or books. You can look at your sales by region and create custom date ranges, so you can see your sales figures for "Today," "Yesterday," the "Last 30 Days" or any custom period that you want.

You can also toggle off and on the *Include Free Titles* switch so that the stats you see on this page either include or exclude any free eBook downloads.

By default, the dashboard sales will be set to *This Month* and will show you the SALES AT A GLANCE view.

At the top you will see a high-level overview that contains stats such as overall number of eBooks sold in that period as well as all-time since you first created your KWL account, your estimated earnings for the period (as well as all-time), the number of books published in that period and the number of countries your books have been purchased in. I can, for example, change my Custom period to the beginning of my Kobo publishing adventure. (That's easy for me. I was the first author account created when the system launched in July 2012). From July 2012 to August 2018 the 21 eBooks I have published have sold titles in 74 countries.

Below that chart is the Top Sellers, ranked up to the top 10 in the same given period you are looking at. Beside it is a Purchase Activity bar chart with the values of "High" and "Low" and "Daily Average" values for that period.

On the bottom left below those two charts is the Top Sellers of All Time chart, which, again, shows your top 10 bestselling titles.

And finally, a fun, and perhaps the most popular feature on the dashboard for many authors is the "Purchase

Activity by Region" map, which basically shows you where in the world people are buying your book. Where-ever people buy your book, there's a blue dot on the map; the bigger the dot, the higher the sales volume.

The dots are created as a representative of the percentage of your sales in that territory for a given time period. If you have sold 2 books in a particular month, for example, and those sales are in the US and Canada, then the two blue dots showing in both those countries on the map would be the exact same size.

Below is an example from my own Kobo Writing Life account dashboard showing sales between January 1, 2017 and August 23, 2018.

You'll notice that the size of the dots over Canada, UK, Australia, New Zealand and the United States are larger in size that the others. This is an easy way to see that, for me, those are the largest markets served by KWL, which Canada being the largest, the UK and the US about even for second and third place, Australia coming in fourth and New Zealand in fifth. South Africa is next. Followed by Taiwan and then Turkey.

If you can't already tell, just pausing to look at the map in the process of writing up this section has resulted in a side-track and delay. And that is one of the down-sides to the analytics available in the dashboard. It can be useful to understand where your books are selling so you can compare that to various promotional and marketing activities you are engaging in. But it can also be a rabbit-hole you might easily fall down. (I mean, let's be honest, looking at where in the world your books are selling is a self-pleasuring activity perhaps akin to mental masturbation).

There are also a SALES BY BOOK and SALES BY REGION.

If you select SALES BY BOOK, you are asked to enter the ISBN or Title for the book in question. Once you start typing, the field will start to show auto-fill suggestions by Title that you can click on. You will get similar basic and overview sales info for that title for a given period, with its own unique map. But one enhancement that doesn't yet appear in the regular SALES AT A GLANCE view is that the *Purchase Activity by Region* listing isn't just the Top 10, but a comprehensive list. I can see, for example, the 51 countries where my anthology *Campus Chills* has sold since I first started publishing it via Kobo Writing Life.

This report is useful for tracking trends on free converting into sales.

For example, *This Time Around* is a short story with a call to action to purchase the full-length novel featuring the same character *A Canadian Werewolf in New York*. I can look at the downloads per country for *This Time Around* and compare it to the sales of the linked title in that series to measure my free to paid conversion. Similarly, *Prospero's Ghost* is a free short story with a call-to-action to purchase the full anthology *Campus Chills*. If I have spent any efforts or money promoting *Prospero's Ghost* during a particular time period, I could look at where I moved a lot of units, and then compare that to the number of sales of *Campus Chills* for a rough free to sales conversion estimate.

It is, of course, a more straight-forward process if you have a series and there is a free first book or free prequel story that you use as a funnel. But I think you get the picture of how those analytics could be used.

Within SALES BY REGION you can determine if there are different titles that do better in a particular country.

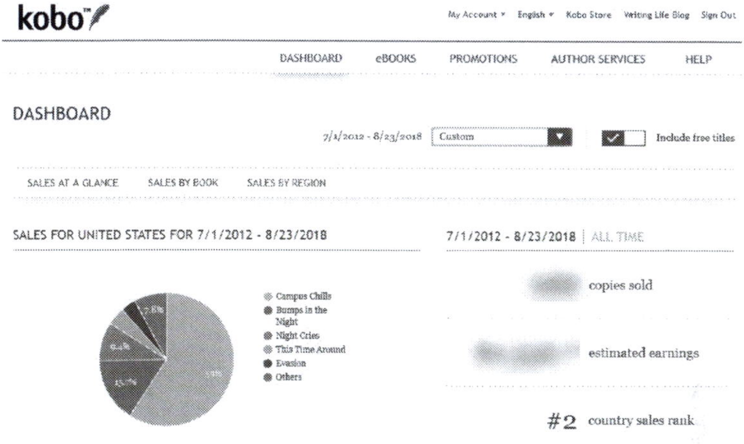

What you can see, when looking at the United States, for example, is that, for me, the US is my second highest selling country in terms of sales rank. (Yes, as you might suspect, Canada is #1 for me and for most other KWL authors). But I can also determine that, in the US, the book *Campus Chills* accounts for 59% of my sales and that *Bumps in the Night* (a mini story collection) is second highest at 15.7% followed by *Night Cries* at 9.4% and *This Time Around* at 4.4%. Since the first two have been published for years, but *Night Cries* is barely a few months old at the time of this report, this suggests a trend that my short fiction collections do better on Kobo in the US than my longer fiction titles like *Evasion*.

This is where, looking at a different country, in this case, Canada, helps me better understand the differences with where different titles sell better.

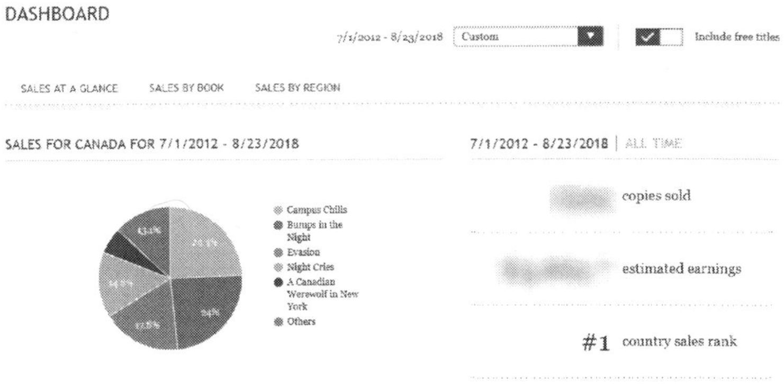

Canada is, as suspected, my #1 country in terms of sales rank. But the title sales spread is little bit more spread out, with the top-selling title, *Campus Chills* again, leading by only a slight margin at 24.4% ahead of *Bumps in the Night* at 24% and *Evasion* (a novel) at 17.8%.

In South Africa, which is my 8th highest ranking country, *Night Cries* accounts for 51.9% of volume. Of course, if I toggle the *Include Free Titles* button to show only actual sales, *Bumps in the Night* is in the lead at 62.5%.

Again, there are some intriguing analytics that can help you understand if one country is nothing but a bunch of free-loading hoarders.

Of course, when you first start (ie, for your first login to that screen), you won't see any sales info or maps with blue dots as you haven't published anything yet. In fact, you won't see any of the actual dashboard, but, instead, a representation of what sort of analytics the dashboard offers you once you start publishing, as well as a prompt to begin the process to publish your first book.

EBOOKS

This is where you can Manage your eBook catalog by adding new titles or editing existing ones.

Here is a quick step-by-step walk through of how to get your book up onto Kobo.

1) Go to the eBOOK tab and hit the *Create new eBook* button

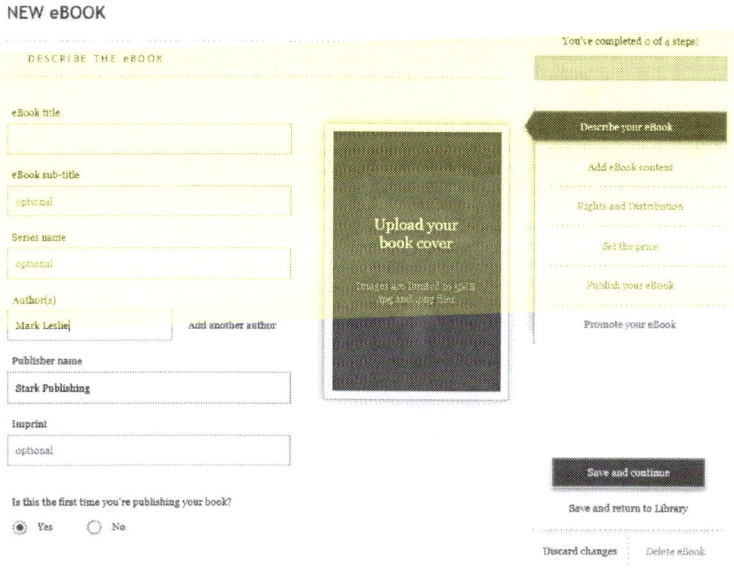

Describe your eBook

On the first screen, called ***Describe your eBook*** you will see the following field options. Any field that is not mandatory will have the slightly faded word "optional" appearing in it.

- **eBook title:** The name of the book. Enter your title exactly as you would like it to appear in the Kobo catalog.
- **eBook sub-title:** The sub-title for the book. Please enter your sub-title exactly as you would like it to appear in the Kobo catalog.
- **Series name:** If your book is part of series, this is where you enter the name of the series.
- **Volume number:** This field only appears if you enter a value into the *Series* name field. Here you enter the book number from your series. (Hint: 0 and decimal values are valid entries here, so you can enter a prequel to a series or even have up to 9 interstitial eBooks between two full volumes in a series. IE, a short story that takes place between Books 1 and 2 in a series might be entered as 1.5)
- **Author(s):** The name of the person(s) who wrote the book. Enter the author's name exactly as you would like it to appear in Kobo's catalog. If you write under a pseudonym, please use that name here. You can add multiple authors by clicking on the red **Add another author** field.

- **Publisher name:** The name of the book's publisher. If you are a self-published author, you can enter your name. If you are an individual doing business as a publisher, you can enter your publisher's name here. (Since first starting my publishing journey in 2004, I have been using the registered business name *Stark Publishing*)
- **Imprint:** The trade name under which your book is published. Publishers may have different imprints to reflect their content types. For a larger publisher like Penguin Random House, they might have hundreds of different imprints. (For someone like me, I only have two different imprints so far. The generic *Stark Publishing* and the *Stark Publishing Solutions* imprint for my non-fiction books on publishing, like this one). This field is a clickable and searchable field on the item pages, so even if your Imprint is the same as your Publisher name, go ahead and fill this out. See below for a view of how the Imprint field shows up in a section at the bottom of the book's item detail page. (This example is from my book *A Canadian Werewolf in New York*)

- **Is this the first time you're publishing your book?** If your book has already been published before you can enter the original publication date here. If you select yes, this field will default to today's date.
- **eISBN:** Kobo's term for the 13-digit ISBN (International Standard Book Number) assigned specifically to the eBook being submitted. Please note that this must be an ISBN that is unique to the eBook version – you can't use the same ISBN that you have for the print version of your book. If you leave this field blank, Kobo will assign your book a *dummy* ISBN that will start with the numbers 1234 and be a valid EAN13 "check-digit" value. Valid and legitimate ISBNs or Bookland EANs that are internationally recognized, will always start with 978 or 979.
- **Primary Print ISBN:** The ISBN associated with the primary print version of your book. If you don't have a print version, leave this field blank.
- **eBook language:** This is the language in which your book is written
- **Synopsis:** A brief description of your book that will appear on your book's item page in the Kobo Store. This might be, for the equivalent of a paperback book, the text that would appear on the back of the book which is a "sales copy" style description. The field allows for basic HTML formatted such as **bold** and *italics*. See an example below, from my book *A Canadian Werewolf in New York.*

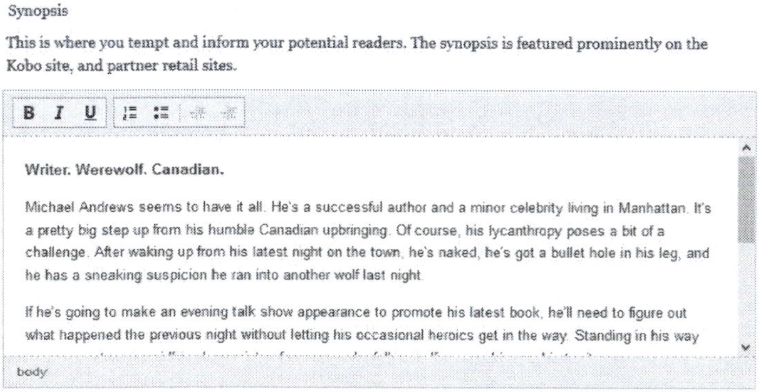

- **Upload your book cover**: If you hover over and then click anywhere in this field, a browser window will open on your desktop allowing you to upload a file. You can upload a .jpg or .png file. Kobo recommends, for best results, that you upload an image with 300 dpi that is no larger than 5 MB
- **Categories:** The categories are the subject categories where a customer might expect to find your book. Think of these like the categories in a bookstore or library. What "aisle" might a customer browse in order to find your book? You can choose up to three categories for your book. When you click on the *Edit Categories* field, a pop-up window will appear allowing you to scroll through and select up to three categories by selecting check-boxes. Below is an example of the categories I use for *A Canadian Werewolf in New York*.

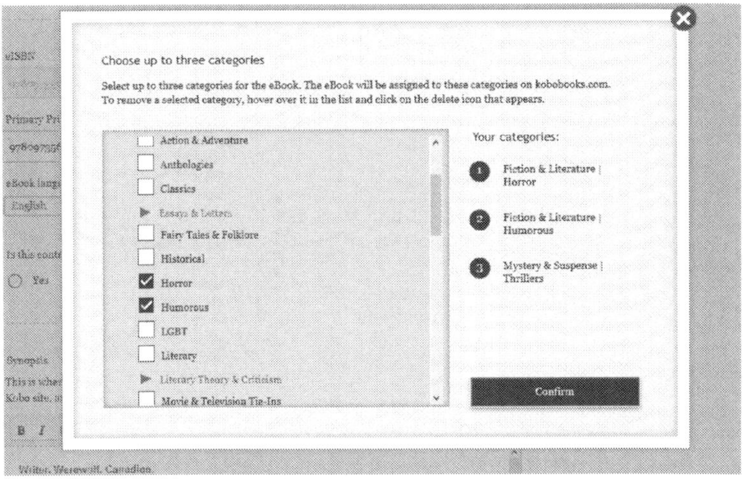

You can remove a category by either de-selecting the check box on the left hand-side, or hovering over the number, which will update to a "delete" icon, and then clicking on it.

Once you have entered all of the mandatory fields you can hit the ***Save and continue*** button, which will take you to the next step, ***Add eBook content.*** If you have not filled out all of the mandatory fields, the ones that you missed will be highlighted in red. See example below of an eBook that is missing the cover and category values.

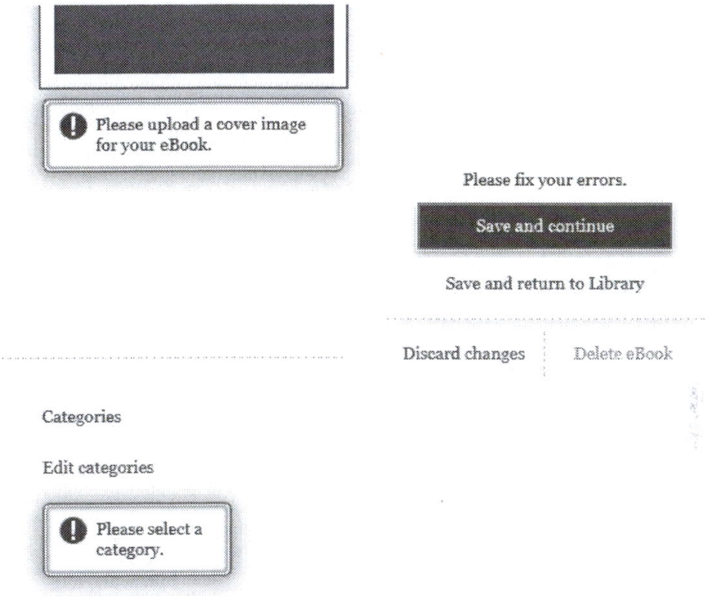

Add eBook content

On the second screen you can upload the content file for your book, or the "interior" of your book in any of the following formats:

- DOC and DOCX
- OPF
- ePub
- MOBI

If you upload a DOC, DOCX, OPF or MOBI file, the system will automatically convert to ePub format. If you want to see how the book was formatted during the conversion process, you can click on the ***Download and preview this eBook***, save the file to your desktop, then use software that reads ePubs (such as Adobe Digital Editions)

This screen also shows you the last time you uploaded or updates your interior content file with a *Last updated* value, which can be useful as you manage revised or updated versions of the book over time.

The VALIDATION RESULTS for the uploaded file will provide you any feedback on errors that the automated ePub system runs on every uploaded eBook. If the book passes all checks, you'll see a message that reads *Your eBook is ready to be published to Kobo's catalog!*

It is possible that your eBook might pass the checks that would allow it to publish to Kobo's catalog, but which would fail if published to OverDrive, Kobo's sister company that distributes to the library market. This means you can publish the book, but will not be able to opt-in to OverDrive library publishing. An example of one such error appears in the screen shot below.

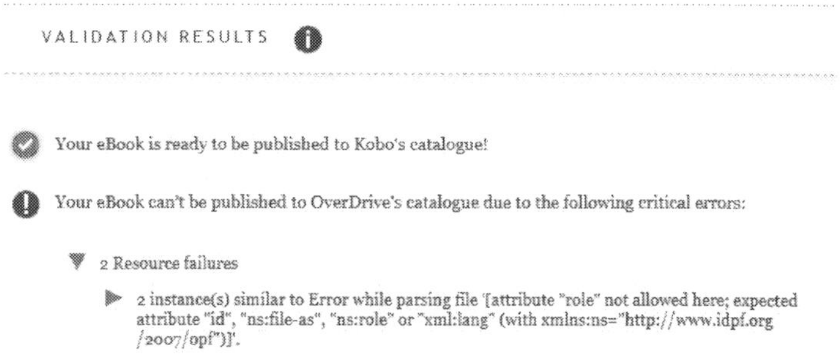

The free eBook conversion tool that Kobo has is not very forgiving, particularly when you are using a Word (DOC or DOCX) file to generate an ePub. If you haven't formatted the Word file exactly to specifications (and there is always plenty of hidden "junk" in a Word document that most users never see), the resulting conversion can be a bit ugly or messy looking or cause some strange formatting issues.

Kobo does recommend that you bring your own perfectly formatted and tested ePub for the best results. There are plenty of professional ePub conversion services available, as well as plenty of free ones as well.

If you own a Mac, I would strongly suggest investing in Vellum (www.vellum.pub) for the most comprehensive and easy experience creating ePubs and Mobi (Amazon's proprietary version of the ePub standard) files. I have yet to meet a writer using Vellum who isn't almost 100% satisfied with their investment and experience.

Since I do not own a Mac, I have learned how to use free programs such as Calibre (https://calibre-ebook.com) and SIGIL (https://sigil-ebook.com) for basic editing of existing valid ePub files and have gotten into the habit of using Draft2Digital.com's free conversion tool, which, in my experience, is the best free Word to ePub/Mobi conversion tool available.

Reedsy also has a free online ePub file creation tool called The Reedsy Book Editor that allows you to not only to write and format a book into ePub and PDF, but there's also the ability for collaboration in terms of working with a co-author or an editor within the tool.

As I've said, there are plenty of options; but you can always use the free built-in conversion tool. Getting the format exactly the way you want does require a little bit of WORD formatting gymnastics, but it most certainly can be done.

Rights & Distribution

This is where you can confirm that you own the rights to distribute your eBook worldwide, choose to make it available to Kobo Plus subscribers (much more on that later on), submit it for library distribution via OverDrive (again, there'll be more on that later) and where you can opt-in to Digital Rights Management.

- **Apply Digital Rights Management:** By default, this box is not checked. Selecting this option adds a lock to the ePub that prevents a customer who buys your eBook from being able to move the file out of Kobo's ecosystem.

Is DRM useful or does it just penalize your honest customers/readers? The debate continues in writing and publishing circles, so I won't get into that here. However, my personal belief is that DRM brings no value to me as an author or to my readers. This is something you need to decide for yourself.

- **Geographic Rights:** By default, the *Worldwi* box is selected. This is because you own the rights to any content that you have written the minute it has been "put on paper." Unless you have sold or licensed all or partial rights to your work to a publisher or agent, you still own world rights and can leave the default *Worldwide Rights* box checked. what about if book has been translated?

If you have sold or licensed rights to your book (for example, if you sold the North America rights to a publisher), you can de-select the *Worldwide Rights* box and then manually remove any of the territories where those rights have been sold. In the same example (see below), the territories for North America have been removed.

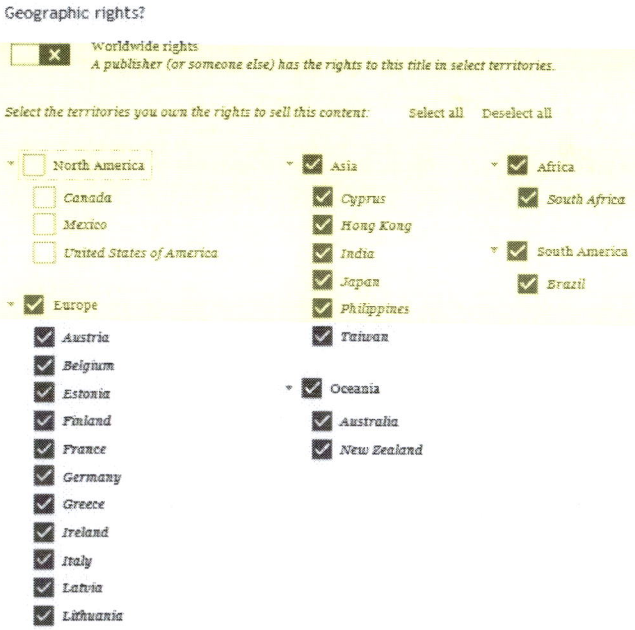

This is becoming more and more common as many of the larger publishers are purchasing only US or only Canadian or only North American rights, which allows authors the flexibility (on both Kobo and Kindle) to publish their own version of the same book in hundreds of other global territories.

- **Make Available with Kobo Plus:** This is where you can choose to have your eBook added to a subscription "all you can read" system that, at the time of this writing, is only available to Kobo and BOL customers in the Netherlands and Belgium. You will get paid whenever more than a particular % of your book is read via this program. Later on, I will share details about the benefits of Kobo Plus. In the meantime, you can learn more about Kobo Plus and how it works at https://kobowritinglife.com/contact-us/about/about-kobo-plus/

- **Make Available to Libraries:** This is where you can choose to make your eBook available to the OverDrive catalog where thousands of different libraries around the world will have access to purchase it. When you choose this option, you are required to enter a unique Library Price in USD. This price is completely independent of your USD price which we will look at in the next main title setup step. But the USD Library Price must be a minimum of $0.99. The KWL team also suggests that your USD Library Price always be slightly higher than your USD Retail Price.

This is because, when a library purchases your eBook, they can loan it to multiple library patrons over time. Later on, I will share more details about how you can benefit from this opportunity for additional income/revenue.

If, during the **Add eBook content** step, you encountered an error that might prevent publication to OverDrive, you will see a notification that states "Your EPUB is not suitable for library use. Please see the content step for more details."

Make Available to Libraries?

Add your eBook to OverDrive's catalogue to enable thousands of libraries around the world to purchase it.

You'll need to set a unique USD library price independent of your USD retail price. The same sales rights shown above will apply to your eBook when sold through OverDrive.

Note that any changes to your eBook, including opting in or out, may take up to a week to be updated in OverDrive's catalogue.

Terms of Service

Your EPUB is not suitable for library use. Please see the content step for more details.

Set the Price

The default list price will be your default currency. My own default currency is CAD because I'm Canadian. If you are from the US you'll most likely set your default to USD. If you're in the UK, to GBP.

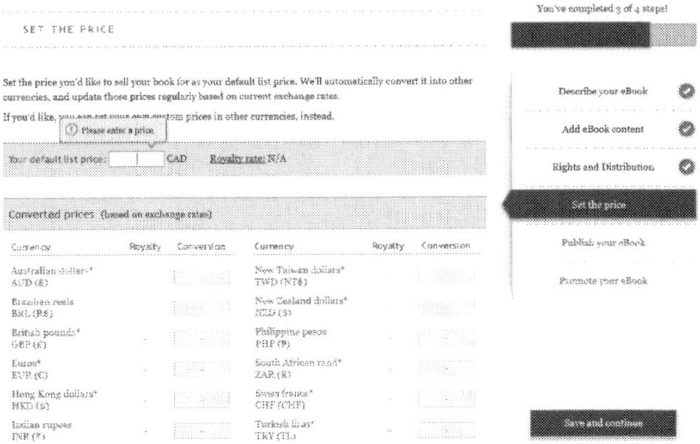

When you enter a price in your default currency, all of the automatically converted prices in the other currencies will populate. In the same screen shot below you see that I entered $4.99 CAD and the corresponding defaults all appear.

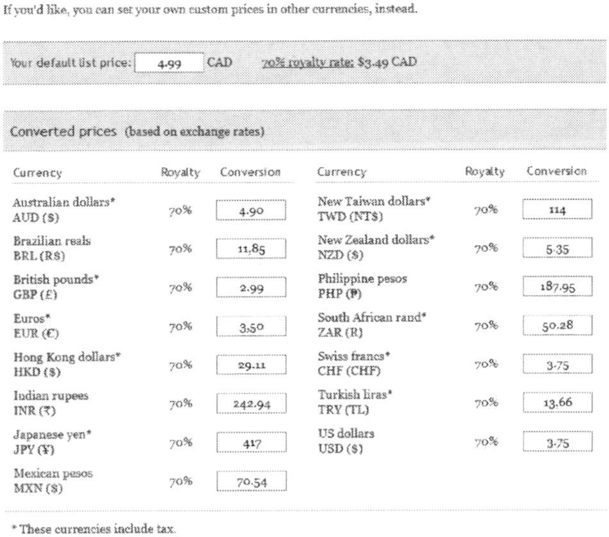
If you'd like, you can set your own custom prices in other currencies, instead.

Your default list price: 4.99 CAD 70% royalty rate: $3.49 CAD

Converted prices (based on exchange rates)

Currency	Royalty	Conversion	Currency	Royalty	Conversion
Australian dollars* AUD ($)	70%	4.90	New Taiwan dollars* TWD (NT$)	70%	114
Brazilian reals BRL (R$)	70%	11.85	New Zealand dollars* NZD ($)	70%	5.35
British pounds* GBP (£)	70%	2.99	Philippine pesos PHP (₱)	70%	187.95
Euros* EUR (€)	70%	3.50	South African rand* ZAR (R)	70%	50.28
Hong Kong dollars* HKD ($)	70%	29.11	Swiss francs* CHF (CHF)	70%	3.75
Indian rupees INR (₹)	70%	242.94	Turkish liras* TRY (TL)	70%	13.66
Japanese yen* JPY (¥)	70%	417	US dollars USD ($)	70%	3.75
Mexican pesos MXN ($)	70%	70.54			

* These currencies include tax.

You can manually adjust any of the prices. When you do, those prices will appear, above in a *Custom Prices (set by you)* field.

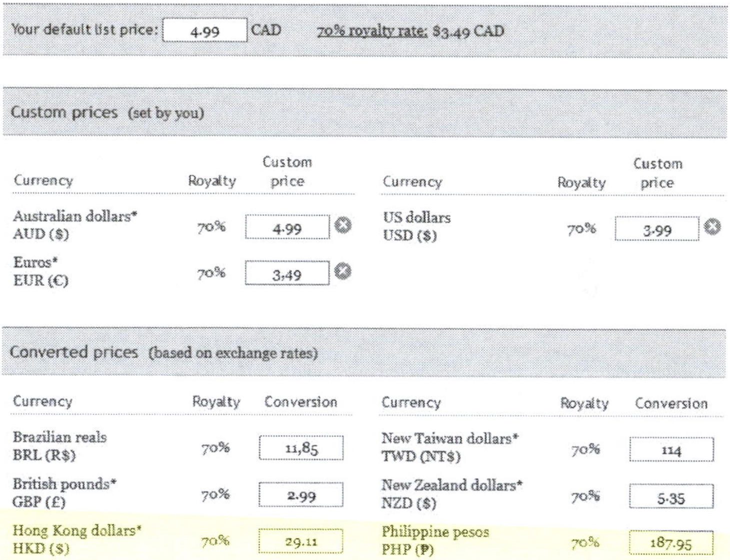

In the chapter *Price Optimization,* I will walk through details and strategies on how you should leverage your ability to manually adjust prices following specific guidelines in order to help maximize and optimize the margin you earn through global sales at Kobo.

I already outlined the basic pricing structure in the *Pricing Structure* differences in the *Ways that Kobo Differs from Kindle* section of the *Kobo 101* chapter, but, for the sake of convenience, I will repeat them below.

Kobo Writing Life authors and publishers receive a 70% or 45% royalty rate on each eBook sold through the

Kobo store. eBooks that are priced according to the following pricing rules are eligible to receive a 70% royalty rate:

- CAD – Canadian Dollar – greater than or equal to $2.99
- AUD – Australian Dollar – greater than or equal to $2.99
- GBP – British Pound Sterling – greater than or equal to £1.99
- EUR – Euro – greater than or equal to €1.99
- NZD – New Zealand Dollar – greater than or equal to $2.99
- HKD – Hong Kong Dollar – greater than or equal to $15.99
- JPY – Japanese Yen – greater than or equal to ¥299
- CHF – Swiss Franc – greater than or equal to 2.99
- TRY – Turkish Lira – greater than or equal to ₺5.99
- BRL – Brazilian Real – greater than or equal to R$7.99
- MXN – Mexican Peso – greater than or equal to $39.99
- TWD – Taiwan Dollar – greater than or equal to $70
- ZAR – South African Rand – greater than or equal to R29.99
- PHP – Philippine Peso – greater than or equal to ₱99.99
- INR – Indian Rupee – greater than or equal to ₹149.99

If your book is priced under any of these values, a sale in that particular territory/currency will result in a royalty of 45% instead of 70%. In the example screen show below, you'll notice that, if I manually adjust the USD price to $0.99 it'll show that I will earn 45% rather than 70% for sales in that currency.

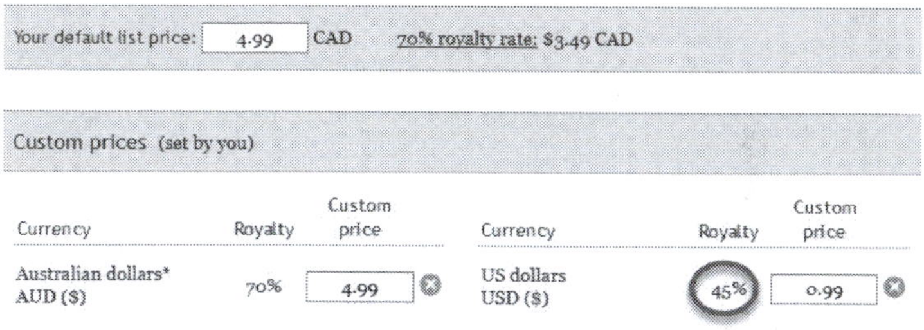

You are also required, by the terms of the agreement to publish via Kobo Writing Life to ensure that your eBook is priced at least twenty percent (20%) lower than the price of the print edition of the book, if one is available. This is a rule that comes via traditional publishing, which I have never seen enforced over the years. And most indie/self-published authors would never overprice their eBook anyway. If anything, I have found that indie authors will typically under-price or under-value their eBooks.

In addition, PUBLIC DOMAIN works are only eligible to receive a royalty rate of 20%.

When you go back in to EDIT an existing book, the ***Set the Price*** screen will show you *Your Custom Prices,* the ability to *Edit Prices* and, below that, the ability to *Schedule a sale* or *Schedule a price change.*

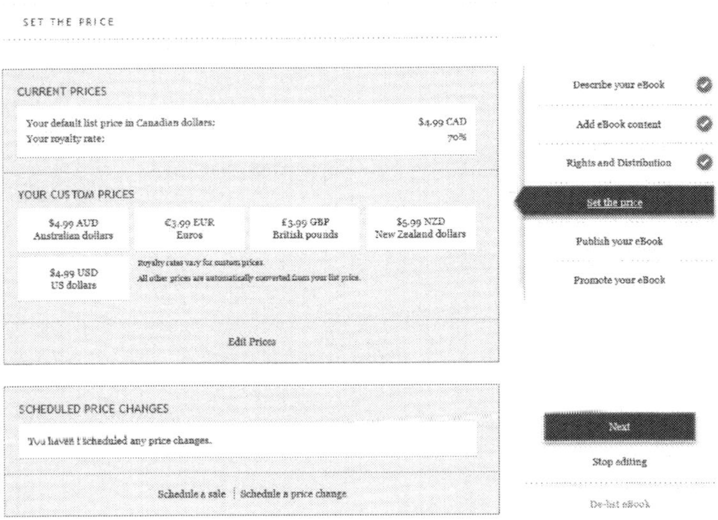

Here's how those fields work:

- **Edit Prices:** If you wish to change your prices immediately, simply click this and make your price changes, then click on *Save*
- **Schedule a sale:** A sale is when your regular price will drop for a limited time and then will, after that time period, return back to the normal/regular price. For example, if your regular price is $4.99 USD and you want to do a week-long sale for $0.99 starting on the first of the next month and then ending on the 7th, you can use this feature to set up that info. The price will automatically change at midnight on the day of the start of this period and then return back to your regular price at the end of that time.

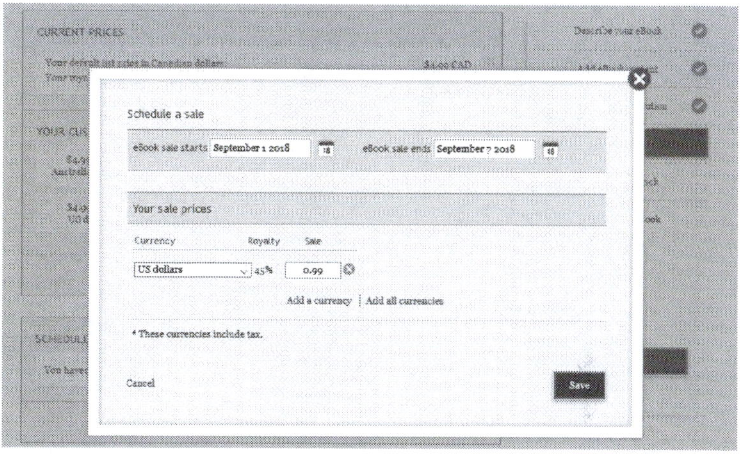

- **Schedule a price change**: To schedule a "permanent" price change in the future, use click on this option and then enter the date that you want the price change to happen. The price will revert on the date you set and remain at that price until you edit/change it again.

For either of these options you can enter a single currency for the change or as many currency changes as you wish.

When a sale price is active in the system, you will see those values under *SCHEDULED PRICE CHANGES* with the start and end date. Similarly, if there is a future price change scheduled, you will be able to see that as well.

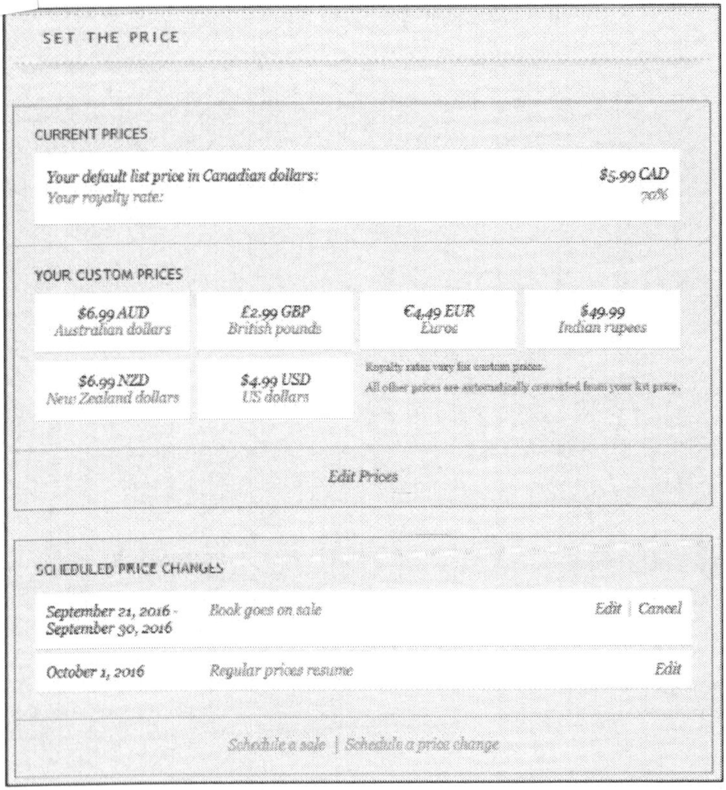

Publish your eBook

As you complete all mandatory fields in each step, a green check-box will appear beside them. Once you enter all data for the four required steps, you'll see the option ***Publish your eBook***.

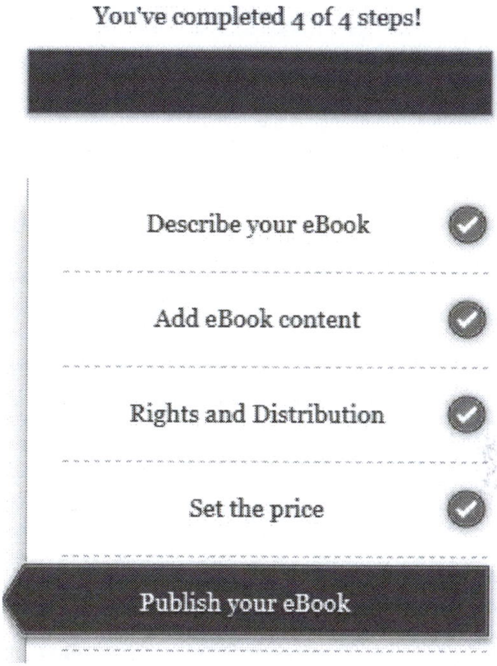

By default, the publication date will be entered as today's date. You can change the date to a different one, and, should you choose a date in the future, you will be asked whether or not you would like to allow customers to pre-order the title.

In the next chapter, entitled ***Optimizing Pre-Order Sales*** I will cover ways you can take full advantage of pre-orders on Kobo.

Also, once you publish the book, you will see the ***Promote Your eBook*** option as a clickable link, and I'll be coming back to that opportunity in the chapter entitled *The Kobo Writing Life PROMOTIONS Tool*).

PROMOTIONS

The next tab that appears (or might not appear) is the PROMOTIONS tab. As mentioned above, there is an entire chapter dedicated to this tab and its function.

The thing that's important to know is you will most likely find this one of the most useful tools inside Kobo Writing Life. The PROMOTIONS tool is often what most KWL authors cite as something that consistently works to help increase their sales at Kobo.

AUTHOR SERVICES

This is an area where you can take advantage of Kobo-negotiated discounts for a number of different publishing related services from trusted partners.

If you don't know where to look for cover design and editorial support, professional eBook formatting, getting reviews for your books, etc, this can be a useful resource.

There's a bit more information about author services in the ***Other Details & Hacks*** chapter.

HELP

Clicking this tab takes you to the HELP & LEARNING CENTRE (yes, "centre" is spelled the Canadian way). This is where you will find:

- An embedded video walk-thru (about 5 minutes) of the basic title setup process for KWL
- A link to a PDF of Frequently Asked Questions (FAQ) for Kobo Writing Life
- A link to a PDF of the Kobo Writing Life User Guide
- A link to a PDF of the Kobo Writing Life conversion guidelines (for formatting your WORD document for optimal conversion to ePub format)
- The CONTACT email for the KWL team (which is writinglife@kobo.com)
- A link to the Kobo Writing Life blog at www.kobowritinglife.com

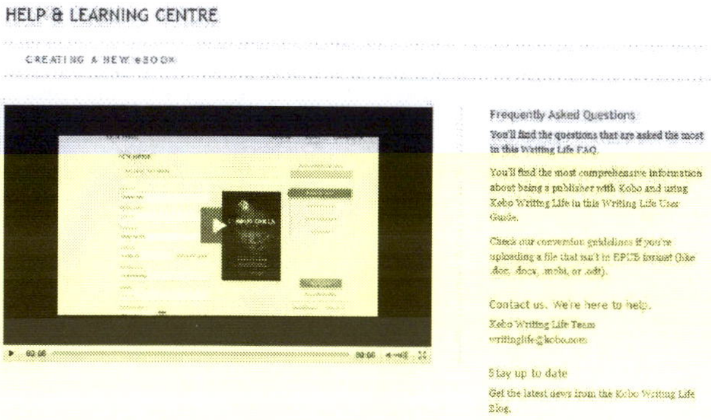

You can also toggle off and on the *Include Free Titles* switch so that the stats either include or exclude any free eBook downloads.

Whew, that was a lot. Let's now think about your forthcoming title at Kobo and how you can optimize those pre-order sales.

OPTIMIZING PRE-ORDER SALES

What Is a Pre-order?

PRE-ORDERS STEM from a pre-internet age when bookstores would place orders for books months in advance of a launch. Publishers would set up display booths at trade shows like Frankfurt Book Fair, London Book Fair and Book Expo America and get bookstore buyers to place orders for upcoming titles. Customers could also leave their name with a local store to secure a copy on the release day.

These days, customers can not only reserve a physical book via orders from online bookstores, but they can have it arrive at their home on the release day. Digital bookselling perfected that art down to a 12:01 AM delivery of the eBook on the day of the book's release.

Pre-ordering has evolved, but its function among retailers remains the same: It gives them an idea of an upcoming book's potential to sell, which then gives them an incentive to promote it.

How Do Pre-orders Benefit Indie Authors on Kobo?

Marketing experts almost always tell authors to set up pre-orders so that they can issue a call-to-action when promoting their books ahead of the launch. "Pre-order now" is a much better call to action than "remember to buy my book in a month's time, okay?"

However, in addition to this generic benefit of pre-orders, on Kobo there are specific additional benefits to optimizing your pre-order strategy:

Give Kobo merchandisers time to consider it

The human beings who curate the online Kobo stores to set up feature pages, carousels and other promotional spotlights (otherwise known as 'merchandisers') are constantly looking for new books to feature in different categories and in different ways. One of the things they keep their eye out for is hot new pre-order top-sellers to spotlight. They plan those features out anywhere from 6 to 12 weeks or more in advance.

For the best chance to feature in one of these spots, you should set your book to pre-order as early as you can — and start working on picking up those early orders!

Double your rankings benefit

Kobo's ranking algorithm works in a similar way to most other online retailers — the more units you sell, the higher your book will rank. Higher ranking books will be shown to more relevant customers (relevancy is based on their browsing history), which can lead to more sales and help sustain that higher ranking.

On Kobo, however, every pre-order sale has TWICE the effect on ranking as a post-launch sale.

Let me repeat that again but using slightly different words.

On Kobo, every pre-order sale has TWICE the effect on ranking as a regular sale.

And, once more, slightly altering the statement and just to ensure we're both on the same page here.

On Kobo, every pre-order sale counts TWICE as much as a regular sale.

When you list your book for pre-sale on Kobo, it will appear on the rankings alongside every other book that is on sale. To maximize visibility on your launch day, you want to accumulate as many pre-order sales in the weeks before release as possible – this will help you take full advantage of this double-bump in rankings.

Here is an example, a screenshot from the Kobo catalog, taken on the week when David Gaughran released his latest marketing book. (I am, of course, using this specific book as an example for a reason – it is a great book and one that I highly recommend)

★★★★☆ (2)

#1 in Nonfiction, Reference & Language, Language Arts, Writing & Publishing, Publishing
#1 in Business & Finance, Marketing & Sales, Advertising & Promotion
#1 in Nonfiction, Health & Well Being, Self Help, Self Improvement, Creativity

You'll notice that David's book is ranking #1 in all 3 of his chosen merchandising categories. He listed the title for pre-order months in advance. And in those months, he marketed the book to his ideal target audience, directing customers towards the pre-order page on all retailers.

By the time this book launched, David had already climbed to the top of his categories on the strength of his double-dipping pre-orders.

Can You Set Your eBook to Pre-order If It Isn't 100% Complete?

Kobo Writing Life requires that you load an eBook before you publish any book — and that includes pre-order titles. If the final version isn't ready, you can get around this by creating a placeholder file with the title page and copyright, and maybe even a non-final draft of the first few chapters of the book.

Because customers can preview the first 5% of an eBook in Kobo's catalog, I always include a short note or introduction from me to the reader at the very front of the book letting them know I'm excited about the new release and that the book is with my editor or some similar description.

In this note/introduction, I also mention that this is a pre-order version and if the customer is reading this particular note after having purchased the eBook and either on or after the release date, then something went wrong with the technology (which can happen). I ask them to email me, as I'd rather fix a poor reader experience than rely on a random customer service rep at Kobo, who might not understand what went wrong and further frustrate my reader.

To provide a concrete example, here's what I did for the pre-release version of the book **The 7 P's of Publishing Success**

First, I created a unique version of the draft with a file name that reminded me this was the special "preview/pre-order" version.

Original file name:
The7PsofPublishingSuccess.ePub

The "Not Yet Ready for Prime Time" Pre-Order File Name:
The7PsofPublishingSuccess_PreOrderVersion.ePub

Second, in that unique version, I inserted a chapter at the very beginning, which should be guaranteed to be seen in preview mode.

Here is the text from that chapter for

NOTE FROM AUTHOR

THIS IS THE PRE-ORDER / PREVIEW VERSION

Please note that if you are seeing this either in preview or as a purchased product, you are reading an early draft / advance reader copy unedited draft version that was loaded to retail websites during the pre-order period while the book was still receiving final edits.

At the stage of this writing, the book is still going through revisions, edits and upgrades with the editorial and design team.

If, for some reason, you received this as a purchased version, then that is the result of some sort of technical glitch or error. To receive the proper version of the book, please email me at mark@starkpublishing.ca and let me know where you purchased it so I can work with that retailer to fix the error and also ensure you receive the proper ePub or mobi (Kindle) version.

Yours in writing,
Mark

It's also the first thing someone sees if, in the case something goes wrong, they have received the wrong/earlier draft version of the book that hasn't gone through the final edit.

Now that we've looked at how to optimize your forthcoming at Kobo's, let's pause to have a look at the people-factor at Kobo and why that's important to understand and to adapt into your marketing and strategy plans.

THE HUMANS BEHIND KOBO AND KOBO WRITING LIFE

UNDERSTANDING THE PEOPLE in any company you work with is important for cultivating relationships, having realistic expectations, and realising where the possibilities lie. This chapter looks at some of the people behind the Kobo Writing Life team.

What Makes Kobo Writing Life Different from Other Retailers?

One of the things that differentiate the Kobo Writing Life team from most of their counterparts is their visibility and accessibility. It has always been a small team, particularly compared to the large volume of business it does. In Nov 2017, Kobo Writing Life sales accounted for a quarter of all books sold at Kobo in English language territories, and one in every five books sold globally).

When you reach out to the KWL team by email (writinglife@kobo.com) or via their Twitter (@KoboWritingLife), Instagram (@Kobo.Writing.Life) or Facebook (@KoboWritingLife) accounts, you'll hear back directly from one of the core KWL team members and not someone in a remote call center.

Meet the Team

When I used to head up the Kobo Writing Life team I always included, in my presentations to authors, a slide of headshots and first names of the entire team. I did this because I wanted to remind authors that behind the systems and the retail site were actual real live people who were passionate about helping authors. Yes, this is something we all already know, but it's so easy, particularly when you are thousands of miles away and frustrated by a system glitch or something that went wrong. It's easy to take it out on the "faceless" corporate goons at Kobo. My desire was a steady and constant reminder of the humans, the faces, the people who were there to support and serve the author community.

The current Kobo Writing Life team is not comfortable with me sharing that information now that I no longer work there, and I completely respect their wishes. Also, because, over time, the team member names and faces change, anything I write here is subject to change and could cause confusion.

For those reasons, I am not posting a picture of the team members nor am I listing the names and roles of the folks on the team. Instead, I will direct you to a post that the KWL team published to their blog in the summer of 2018.

http://bit.ly/ThePeopleBehindKWL

I imagine that, as things change, they will likely either update this specific post, or share that information on their blog. [In fact, I noticed, during a re-edit of this text, that they did just that, with a Sept 2018 article introducing their latest Author Engagement Intern to the world]

The majority of the KWL team that deal with English language books are located in Toronto (the same time zone as New York) where Kobo's main office is location, so most of your responses will come during those business hours. Two of the team members are in Europe, and they typically deal with French, Italian and other non-English language requests.

When you hear back from KWL, it'll most likely be from a KWL Intern or a KWL Author Engagement Coordinator. Technical ePub and metadata processing tickets get assigned to the Publisher Operations members of the KWL team.

If you listen to the Kobo Writing Life podcast you'll hear directly from KWL Director Christine, and Stephanie (from Publisher Operations), who regularly interview authors and offer tips for successful self-publishing. Sometimes, hearing a person's voice is a great reminder of the person behind the title/role.

Why is it important to know the team?

As I've mentioned before, one of the key benefits of Kobo is that the stores are still merchandised by members of a team. The role of the merchandising and promotions lead on the team is specifically responsible for working through the Kobo Writing Life catalog titles and hand-selecting books to feature and present to the larger Kobo merchandiser team, as well as to find promotional opportunities for KWL-authored titles and helping self-publishing authors sell more books!

I'm not exaggerating when I say that having a healthy rapport with the KWL team will come in mighty handy down the line.

Interacting with the Team

It's true to say that most authors only get in touch with the KWL team when something goes wrong. As you interact and communicate, remember that they, like you, are real people and not robots. If you provide as much information as possible about your issue and remain polite, it can save you a lot of time and frustration.

Instead of only contacting the team when there's an issue, consider reaching out with something else:

- Perhaps offer a tip or a suggestion for something you might like to see in the dashboard
- Share an article about something that worked nicely for you on Kobo that might help other authors that they could use on their blog
- Send a tweet out to brag about where in the world you are selling on Kobo using the hashtag #KWLMap

Here is an example of a tweet I sent that got shared and prompted other authors to show their own global sales maps for May.

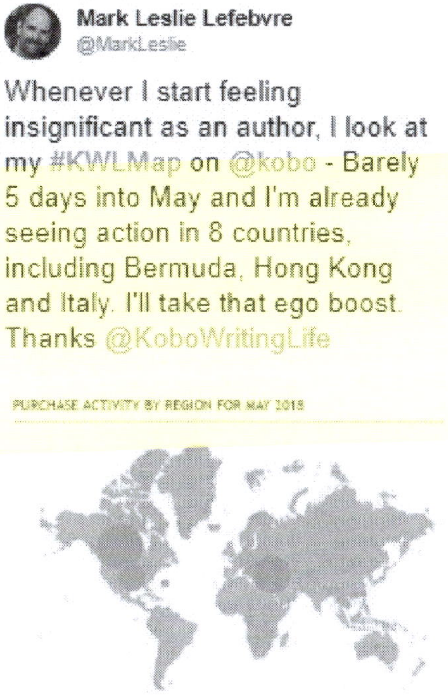

When you do this, it will be almost certainly be seen by the team at Kobo who will be impressed and flattered that you took the time to share something positive and which promotes Kobo's global presence. Because – let's be honest – most authors don't.

The KWL team shared and responded to each of those #KWLMap tweets in May and continues to do so. Of course, in that first week after sending my tweet, I only saw half a dozen authors share their maps, of the more than 70,000 authors on the platform.

Do you think those 6 authors perhaps stand out to the KWL team?

The Other Humans at Kobo

While most of your interactions as an author at Kobo are likely to be with the Kobo Writing Life team, it's important to remember that there are hundreds of other people at the company that support and work alongside that team.

It's important to remember that the KWL team very likely wants the same things you do, but that, because a task, tool or procedure can involve juggling responsibilities and priorities from different perspectives, it might take what seems – from the author's point of view – an unreasonable amount of time.

For example, a simple update to the finance tab to allow authors the ability to download their historic sales data was something that I had originally wanted to put into place back in late 2012. But it only became a reality in early 2018.

The request not only involved significant work from three teams (the development team, the finance team and the web team), but it also included coordinating those tasks among the arms-length list of higher priorities that each of those teams are constantly working on.

What might seem to be a simple request could involve many moving parts, particularly in a larger sized organization. Sometimes, getting traction can only happen after a significant amount of time and effort have been spent.

Though Kobo Writing Life has someone responsible for curating and spotlighting KWL titles into the main merchandising spots, it's important to remember that the merchandisers are receiving requests from thousands of publishers around the world, all competing for that prime retail merchandising space in the digital "front of store." I'll talk about that more in the chapter about promotions.

And I know that I talked about this in the introductory section of the book, but the humans who work at Kobo are guided by some underlying principles that I am still very proud to have been a part of.

Beautiful Book Nerds

Michael Tamblyn, for example, the company's CEO, is one of the most beautiful book nerds I have ever known. And yes, I'm stealing that term from Michael, who used it brilliantly in a presentation at a tech forum in Toronto many years ago to describe the audience, as he saw it, from the stage.

There is an essence known as "Kobo Blood" that exists within the culture at Kobo. Part of it is related to the passion and love of reading. Michael does an excellent job of leading the entire Kobo team with these principals and which are encapsulated wonderfully in a talk that he gave in London in 2015 at the *FutureBook* conference.

Below is an abridged excerpt from that talk.

This is certainly about the reader. We spent a lot of time today talking about the reader. The Reader with a capital R. We are trying to understand the reader. We are, all of us, clustered around the reader, trying to figure out what makes them tick. It's very crowded around the reader right now.

Some of us are analysts, market researchers, statisticians. And we know that there is no one reader; there are lots of different kinds in all shapes and sizes. We segment them and study them. Collect all kinds of data about them. Every once in a while we capture one in the wild and bring it back to the lab and study it. We stand around like scientists saying, "Hmm. What does it eat? Why isn't it moving? Give it an e-book at 99p — oh now it's moving. How about a print-digital bundle? Nope, not so much. Now poke it with a stick. Hmm, interesting." (Health and safety tip: don't poke the readers.)

Some of us are publishers. Publishers will often say: "Our goal is to get as close as possible to the reader, to understand what they want, and to have constant, direct contact with them." Which sounds fine but also, when repeated over and over in an intense and focused way starts to sound vaguely, I don't know — stalker-ish

So publishers: here's a test to determine if your desire to know the reader is making you sound creepy. It's a very simple test. Replace the word "reader" with "Taylor Swift."

For example, if you said: "Our goal is to get as close as possible to Taylor Swift, to understand what Taylor Swift wants, and to have constant, direct contact with Taylor Swift." Things will not go well for you. Not at all. So, don't be a stalker.

But publishers have admired the reader from afar for so long, now they are hoping to a chance to get close.

You want to know as a publisher because you want so much from the reader.

If you're a publisher you want them to love all of your titles, your authors, your spring catalog, your backlist. You dream, deep down, that maybe they might even love you as a publisher, just for being a publisher, you could be a brand, and you could have a line of coffee mugs with your book covers on them, just like those ones from Penguin that you both love and quietly resent.

Now of course if you're a retailer you want so much from the reader too — you want them to discover you, buy from you. You want it to be just like the end of the romance novel — the one where you'll stay together for as long as you both shall live, reading happily ever after. You don't want it to be like the erotic novel — a series of empty encounters, hopping from one retailer's app to the other, an orgy of choice at the expense of happiness and commitment. Retailers want a relationship. We retailers are, when you look at it, shockingly needy. Buy one thing from us and we're like the crazy person who you go on a first date with who then texts you 18 times in 24 hours. "Thanks for signing up. How about an app? Have six bookmarks. Here's 10% off. Here are some recommendations. What's your favourite colour? How do you feel about a June wedding?"

We all—publishers, retailers, authors—want a lot from the reader. And as a result, we think a lot about what readers want. And I mean that very specifically. What they want. What is the next book? The next author. The recommendation, the acquisition, the new category, price point, cover. And the fight to be better at knowing what a reader wants has us occasionally acting like scientists or stalkers or needy boyfriends. Because it's an important question to ask—the essence of publishing and book selling.

But when you think about it, our real fight right now is not to find the next book. Now books compete against everything else. There are more and more things trying to answer: "What else could you be doing now?" So I suggest that we need to ask a different question. I suggest that "how" is just as important. How we read. The quality of that experience, how we read — the need that it satisfies. "What" determines what fills the time. How determines whether we give it any time at all.

So if I take off my retail hat and my e-book hat and my device manufacturer hat and just think of myself as a reader, a few ideas come to mind. They aren't a reader's bill of rights. They aren't a manifesto. They aren't a magna-biblio-carta. They are how we want reading to be.

I picked five.

1. Easy. *We want everything related to reading to be easy, frictionless, even relaxing. What you're reading doesn't have to be easy, but whether it's escape or information, reading is an enjoyable act. Being in a bookstore is a soothing thing. Being in an online bookstore or an e-reader should be too. It shouldn't just be the reading of a book that makes you feel better. The buying of one should make you feel better even before you start reading. Everything that surrounds a book should be easy.*

2. Shamelessly. *We want to feel good about what we read. Forget about guilty pleasures. The great gift of digital reading is the liberation from the judgey person on the tube looking sideways at my fiction choice that is covered in rocket ships or exploding aircraft carriers or low-cut bodices or an embossed photo of David Cameron. We love what we love and that should be the end of it. And we want to feel good about what we don't read. Or half read. Or read three chapters of and then abandon. We're grown-ups. We don't have to eat our vegetables. Books don't have vitamins in them. We can have extra dessert at every meal! It's okay. We want to read shamelessly.*

3. Freely. *And I don't mean in cost. We want time. Time to read. We fight for time. Finding time to read in* *the midst of this distracting world of work and kids and social media and smartphones and TV is like trying to wash your hair while sharing a bathtub with live octopi. It can be done, but requires inventiveness, agility, and great effort. (Waterproof Kobo Aura H2O on sale now at WH Smith, Argos and other fine retailers.) We want more time to read freely.*

4 and 5. Publicly and privately. *We want to talk about what we are reading unless we really don't want to talk about what we are reading. To be able to maintain a public reading life and a private one. Sometimes you'll run into someone who says: "I live out loud. I'm a social reader. I post everything to GoodReads to enrich my social connections and society as a whole." No you don't, you big liar. It's like Facebook. You post the photo of the sweetly beautiful hand-made Christmas card that your five-year-old made you out of glitter and pasta. You don't post any photos about the same child shoving a raisin in his ear and your attempts to extract it with eyebrow tweezers. Books are the same. You post the books that make you look like this intoxicating mix of smart and awesome and sexy. You don't post that every time your boss gives you an especially hard time at work, you re-read Bridget Jones's Diary, which means you have read it 72 times. (And it is not true that I speak from personal experience on that.) We want to be helped but not intruded on. We want to share and hold back.*

Easily, Shamelessly, Freely, Publicly and Privately.

Five ways to answer how we want to read. I picked these five — I'm sure there are others. There should be. But it's a good place to start.

This is a bit of a pivotal FutureBook, in a way. It's about the end of the beginning. We now have four ways to sell a book — bricks-and-mortar, print online, audiobook, e-book. None of them are going anywhere. And each of them gives us a nearly infinite list of options to answer the question "What should I read next?" But from now on, when I feel like I'm being too much of a scientist, or a stalker or a needy boyfriend, I'll ask how readers want to read. The reader's wants are so fundamental, so basic, that they sometimes get lost. They are hard to quantify and obstinately resistant to analysis. But if we answer them well, we earn the right to the reader's attention, we elbow out all of the other media that is crowding in, we get to keep doing what we love to do. And so do they.

This slightly abridged version of that 2015 talk from Michael should give you an idea of the behind-the-scenes at Kobo and of the perspective that Rakuten Kobo's leader has.

If you ever have the chance to meet Michael Tamblyn or to hear him speak about his love for books and for reading, you'll see and feel it immediately.

What I also like about this speech is that it not only portrays some of the underlying DNA of Kobo itself, but it also encapsulates the heart of so many of the people who work in publishing and in book retailing.

A fantastic reminder that we are all in this together with the ultimate goal of bringing the reader and the writer together.

It's the people.

Always the people.

An important thing to always keep in the back of your mind.

Now that we know a bit more about the people behind the company as well as how to optimize our pre-order sales, let's take a look at where in the world you can expect to see the highest sales numbers as well as what categories sell the best on Kobo.

KOBO'S GLOBAL SALES AND BESTELLING CATEGORIES

IN THIS CHAPTER we'll take a look at the global territories with the highest volume of sales, and trends in what sells best at Kobo. As previously mentioned in chapter *Kobo 101*, though Kobo is a Canadian operated and founded company, it is an international retailer and they spent a significant amount of time and effort on a fundamental strategy: Global expansion via local retail partnerships.

One of the reasons Kobo did this is that Amazon already had a significant foothold in the US market with Kindle. Kobo's initial partnership in the US was an attempt to partner with the American Booksellers Association (ABA), which oversaw thousands of independent bookstores across the country as well as a partnership with one of the US's two largest book chains, Borders.

The ABA was already in a partnership with Google Books and wasn't interested in working with Kobo. And Borders went out of business.

Although Google dropped their partnership with the ABA and the CBA (Canadian Booksellers Association), Kobo was there, in the same way that, in the old *Archie* comics, Betty was always there for Archie whenever Veronica had had enough of him and tossed him out. Kobo and ABA developed a system where loyal indie bookstore customers could buy eBooks and still support their favorite local book shop. Via *an Indieboung.org* program and code that could either be embedded into their own site, or merely directed directly to the Kobo US store, a customer could shop for their eBooks, powered by Kobo, with a portion of any eBook they buy being funneled back to the bookstore.

But, by then, it was too late. Kindle dominated the US market in eBook sales and a large segment of early adopter eBook readers owned Kindle devices and were committed to that investment and the Amazon Kindle eBook ecosystem.

Thus, while many in the United States might not be as familiar with the Kobo brand, or, if they are, they feel it is a tiny brand, the same view is not shared in other parts of the world.

Understanding where the Kobo brand, and Kobo sales are stronger can give authors a leg up in terms of where to focus or spend their marketing dollars.

Where Are the Highest Volume of Sales at Kobo?

As shared in ***Kobo 101***, Kobo was born in Canada. So, it is no surprise that, for English language titles, the majority of the sales would be coming out of Canada. The United States, the UK, Australia and New Zealand usually round up the top five.

The information I am sharing below is something that was regularly and consistently shared publicly at writer conferences during my six years as Director of Kobo Writing Life.

While I can make no claims that the data is consistent with the sales of today, based on the sales tracking from my own KWL account as well as the accounts of several writer friends and authors coach and mentor, who either have allowed me direct access to their accounts or have shared, in depth, details of where their sales volumes are, I see evidence that a similar trend is continuing.

The only thing that I suspect is likely to happen is, with the recently new Rakuten partnership with Walmart, the Walmart eBook shop powered by Rakuten Kobo is likely to bring in a new flux of eBook reading customers who aren't already locked into Amazon's ecosystem and will have the effect of further growing the US market for Kobo.

The chart below shows the highest volume of sales from Kobo Writing Life as of the third quarter of 2017 and was taken from multiple presentations I had given when I was Director of KWL.

Where in the World? The 12 Top-Selling Territories on Kobo

50.68% - Canada
11.07% - United Kingdom
10.71% - Australia
9.06% - United States
4.04 % - France
3.00% - New Zealand
2.99% - Rest of World*
2.19% - Italy
1.31% - Netherlands
1.23% - Germany
0.99% - South Africa

** "Rest of World" represents hundreds of territories (about 150) that don't have their own unique merchandised store that is customized to the local country or currency and are, instead, merchandised as a generic store in US dollars.*

Contrast the numbers above with the two main countries most authors see Kindle sales in (US and UK) to get an idea of the breadth of global reach that exists in publishing wide.

In recent years, Kobo has seen an increase in eBook sales across Europe and other non-North American territories, which lines up with what other retailers are experiencing.

However, please take note that these values are spread across a significantly large base of KWL published titles, and that each individual author accounts and sales per title, might differ.

For example, if I were to look at one of my oldest and best-selling titles by volume, *Campus Chills,* which has historical sales in 51 territories on Kobo, I can see that my sales ranking actually has the following:

50.00% - United States
18.69% - Canada
17.36% - UK
3.82% - Australia
2.72% - Netherlands
0.87% - New Zealand
0.51% - Germany
0.41% - Philippines
0.41% - Spain
0.41% - Finland
0.37% - France
0.37% - Malaysia

The prominence of US sales in this particular case is likely due to an early BookBub feature I ran on this title in 2013 which was heavily US-dominated back then, and dramatically shifted US sales into the Pole Position.

If I were to look at *Bumps in the Night,* another one of my older and better-selling titles (and this one a mini-short story collection of about 12,000 words), you'll see this trend:

50.00% - Canada

19.67% - United Kingdom
12.73% - United States
5.73% - Japan
3.55% - Australia
3.34% - New Zealand
0.80% - Israel
0.74% - Singapore
0.69% - Thailand
0.48% - South Africa

A look at the top 10 territories for sales of my novel, *Evasion* reveals the following global spread:

50.00% - Canada
31.39% - Australia
7.88% - United Kingdom
3.88% - United States
2.85% - New Zealand
2.28% - Ireland
0.34% - Singapore
0.34% - South Africa
0.23% - France
0.23% - Belgium

As I was putting these numbers together, I noticed that the top territory for each is sitting at exactly 50%. I was initially thinking that this had to be a complete coincidence, but I pulled and ran numbers for 3 other titles and found that my top-performing territory (always Canada) was exactly 50%. I was wondering if that meant anything, since I'm not an analyst by trade, so I kept digging and found other titles with not as high of a volume, which revealed a different top value. *One Hand Screaming* for example had Canada at 69.57% and *Tricky Treats* shows top territory Canada at 58.82%.

So, apart from the strangeness of Canada being an even 50% in some of my higher selling titles, there is a consistent pattern of Canada being dominant.

What Genres/Categories Sell the Best?

If you are already familiar with the top-selling categories on Kindle or other eBook platforms, then these stats shouldn't come as much of a surprise; nor should the fact that genre fiction far out-sells most other categories.

#1 - Romance
#2 - Mystery/Thriller/Suspense
#3 - "More Active Romance" (AKA Erotica)
#4 - Fiction
#5 - Fantasy
#6 - YA
#7 - Sci-Fi

While the actual percentages aren't shared here, the top-selling genres far out-sell the lower ones, even on the top-selling list. If percentages were shown, the sales might look more like the traditional "hockey stick" style slope. Romance, for example, might sell between 5 to 10 times as much as science-fiction.

One trend that has been prevalent in 2016 and 2017 and which seems to be continuing is the growth of mysteries, suspense and thrillers. In the same way that a blockbuster hit like *Fifty Shades of Gray* had an echo effect on the sale of erotica, blockbuster thrillers like *Gone Girl* and *Girl on the Train* have rippled down to increase sales of that category, elevating it to the #2 spot.

If you are writing in a category outside the ones listed below, don't despair. It doesn't mean that there is nobody reading in your category. It just means that it's critical for you to focus on your target audience.

Additionally, one of the trends that we noted was how Kobo's global retail partners can have an affect on what genres or titles sell in higher volumes. Based on stats that both Kobo Writing Life and Kobo's Michael Tamblyn have publicly shared over the years, there is a higher incidence of literary/contemporary fiction as well as more academic/social-science non-fiction titles sold through Kobo's US partnership with the ABA independent bookstores.

There appears to be an interesting relationship between the types of books that customers of independent book shops buy and those sales. While those sales do include the blockbuster titles that takes almost every retailer by storm, they also include more of those "hand-selected" and "curated" titles that a local bookseller might spend a great deal of time hand-selling to their customers.

For an additional look at trends in global sales, it is useful to look at information from Data Guy in the semi-regular *Author Earnings* reports that have been shared over the years. Just bear in mind that the majority of his data focuses on Amazon (which can be limited to a US- or US-and-UK-centric view), and that sales trends on Kobo might be similar, but that they often involve a mix from many more global territories.

An article about the January 2018 Author Earnings report appears here:

http://bit.ly/AuthorEarningsJan2018

The article offers hearty insights that are worth taking into consideration. However, I'd like to call attend to two important takeaways from it:

1) eBook sales are continuing to grow, and to grow globally, despite cries from larger publishers that eBook sales are declining
2) Indie Published and small-publisher eBooks are continuing to capture more of the market away from traditional publishers

Now that we have taken a look at the global territory spread of the sales at Kobo, we can better understand unique-to-Kobo pricing strategies that leverage this knowledge in the next chapter.

PRICE OPTIMIZATION

IN THE PREVIOUS chapter, we looked at what types of books sell in the highest volume as well as the different countries that Kobo performs best in for the average Kobo Writing Life author. That's a good base to have as we now examine ways you can optimize your global pricing in order to maximize your revenue earnings.

Before we talk about specifics I wanted to remind you to keep something in mind. KWL and KDP allow you to control your price in multiple territories. So does a third party distribution like Draft2Digital.

If you look at the clause of your KWL contract, as well as the clause of your KDP contract (not to mention the clauses for Nook, iBooks, etc), you'll see a very consistent clause or term across all of them.

You cannot have a lower price on any other retailer.

Thus, your pricing in USD, in CAD, etc., must be the same across all retail platforms.

Here's a quick look at the Kobo Writing Life Terms of Service that mentions this:

In SECTION 4 of the contract (as of the Sept 19, 2016 update, which is the one showing in the summer of 2018 as I write this), there is a line that reads:

"The SRP for your eBooks provided to Kobo must be less than or equal to the lowest price provided by you to any third party."

Kobo, like Amazon, and Apple and Barnes and Noble, have a clause that says your price can be higher on other platforms, but it cannot be lower. If it is lower, they reserve the right to manually adjust your price to match the lowest price.

Amazon is, the only company that aggressively pursues this using powerful auto-bots. But the contract you signed means you can't over-price your books on Kobo while making them cheap on Kindle.

If your price is $2.99 USD on Kindle, they, by contract, it should be $2.99 USD on Kobo. Otherwise you are in violation of the contract.

Thus, as I'm talking about different prices and different currencies in this section, keep in mind that you can and should make the same changes across all retailers. (With a few exceptions – Kindle doesn't allow for NZD pricing, whereas KWL and Draft2Digital do)

Price Should Be Active, Not Passive

The first thing to remember about pricing stems from advice I heard from Nathan Maharaj – *Senior Director of Merchandising* at Kobo – during an industry presentation he gave to publishers.

Nathan said that price is a verb, not a noun. Price is an action that we take, rather than a noun that we define.

He was referring to the importance of experimentation with price, of trying and testing different price points, and of understanding that pricing is a dynamic factor in a book's metadata.

Price is something that needs to be done strategically, not willy-nilly.

Authors and publishers put a great deal of effort into their book's cover design as well as into their synopsis or blurb in order to maximize the appeal to their target readers. But they need to put as much care and consideration into the price point that they choose.

Nathan went on to suggest the following three things that were important considerations when setting a price.

- **Price Deliberately:** Make sure that you have a plan related to your price and be prepared to measure the results of that plan.
- **Price Responsively**: Pay attention to the market and be prepared to react to changes as the market evolves.
- **Price Often**: Considering both the market changes as well as your pricing plans, remember that price isn't something you set and forget. You can change it.

The three points above aren't meant to suggest that you should be going in and changing your pricing every day. It is meant to help you reflect upon and consider the following when you think about price.

Think about what your regular price should be, based upon considerations like genre and country. But then also consider if you want to have a different launch price strategy, and for what purpose? Will you have a different front-list price and back-list price? Think about newly released digital movies that are priced really high, then, over time, how the price drops significantly. Yes, this is based on a physical distribution world, but consumers are used to that happening across other product lines. A new phone or new game system is priced higher when first released (unless there is a temporary, "buy-now" launch price to entice new consumers), and then the price typically slides down over time as it becomes a backlist product and newer products are now available. But, of course, that's one methodology. Perhaps your own pricing strategy involves very specific price points based on the number in a series you have, to create a funnel for readers.

Unless your goal is to move a lot of units and not earn a sustainable income on your eBook sales, the goal with pricing should usually involve maximizing your revenue.

Seeing How Your Price Looks in Other Countri

By default, when you visit www.kobo.com you will see the currency of the country that you are in. For example, I am in Canada, so Kobo will show me the "Canadian" merchandised version of the store in Canadian dollar pricing. If you are in the United States, you'll see the merchandised "US" store and USD pricing.

Unlike Amazon, that uses the .com, .ca, .de, etcetera. domains, Kobo uses .com but naturalizes the "storefront" based on the customer's account or IP address.

But you can easily see how the UK store looks if you are in the US, for example, quite easily.

When on the Kobo site, look at the top right hand-side of the screen. You'll see a country flag icon. In the screen shot below, it is a US flag, which means I am looking at the US store.

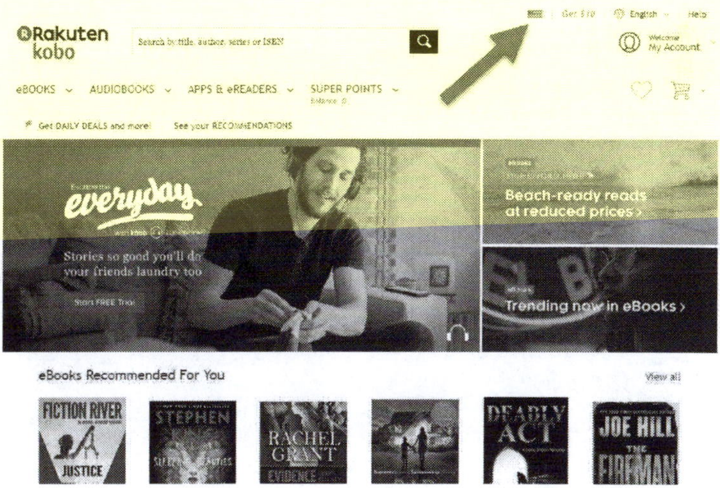

If you click on that country flag icon, it'll bring you to a *Select your country or region* screen where you can alter the country you are looking at. (You won't be able to purchase from a store outside your home territory, but at least you will be able to see what it looks like.)

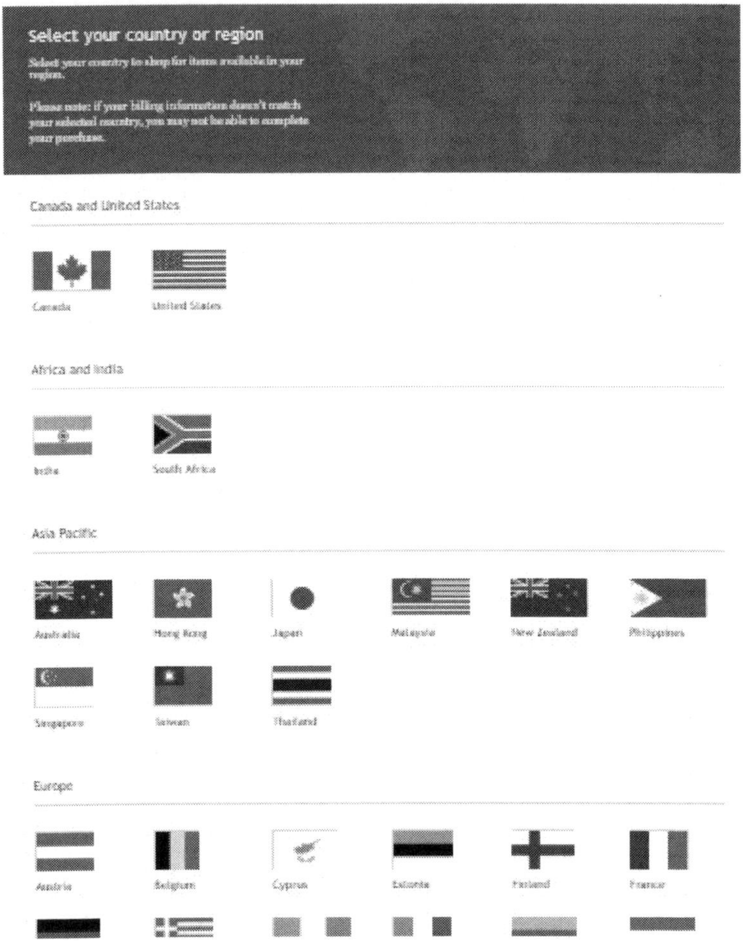

In the screen shot below, which is what I saw after I clicked on the Canadian flag, to bring me back home, you'll notice a few differences about the "storefront" – While there is a large banner pushing audiobooks in both the US and CA stores, the side banners, showing featured promos, are different. Also, interestingly, the *eBooks Recommended for You* are altered a bit.

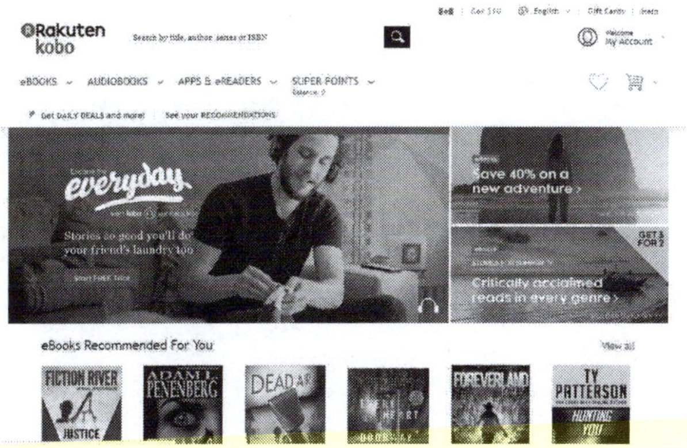

If I click on the Great Britain flag, I'll see, again, a different configuration of the banners, depending on the features and promos the merchandising team is running in the UK.

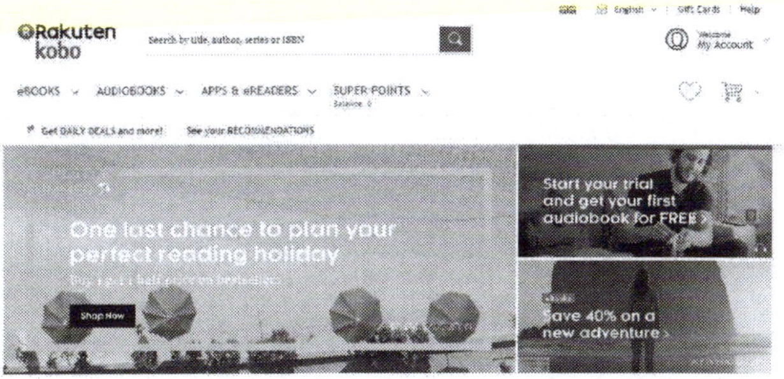

If I click on the flag for the Netherlands, I'll see the what the Dutch site looks like. (Notice the focus on Kobo Plus, the subscription reading program Kobo launched with BOL – there'll be more about that in the chapter ***Additional Revenue Opportunities via Kobo Writing Life***)

It is useful to use this feature on www.kobo.com to understand the different promotions, the different storefronts, and, specifically as part of this chapter, the different prices in global territories.

As you try to determine the best optimal price (something we'll be getting into next in this chapter), this is a handy feature to take advantage of.

Where to Start on Price

When authors ask me to make a recommendation on price, I usually tell them to look at two specific factors: *Category/Genre* and *Comparable Paperback Price*. I then add onto that what I call *Personal Price Factor*.

I use all three of these things to determine a price.

Below I will talk about my reasoning behind look at each of them as well as walk through an example of how I would use that on one of my books.

Price Factor One: Category/Genre

In my own experience as a bookseller, understanding the market you are selling into, and your target audience/reader/consumer is important. If you are writing a technothriller, for example, it's good to look at the top-selling 25 or 50 technothrillers and see what the average eBook price is for those.

Why? They are, as of the day you are looking, the most popular and top-selling books in that category. More people are buying those books in that category than any others. Thus, the author or publisher is doing something right.

Just a quick aside on that. Yes, admittedly, if the author's name is a house-hold recognizable one like Stephen King, J.K. Rowling, James Patterson, then the publisher can likely charge a ridiculously high and unreasonable price and there are enough millions of fans who won't care how much it costs because they know they *have* to read it. (Never forget that – if you don't already have them, there will be fans who feel the same about your writing. So, think about them, and when you have that kind of loyal fan-base think about a **FAIR** price that isn't too high but also isn't under-cutting your ability to earn decent margin and sustain your life as a writing professional). Because, remember, the fact is that those books *are* selling, meaning there are consumers willing to pay that price. That's good to understand.

So, look at the average selling list price in a genre/category in a particular currency. If I were to use a personal example, let me look at the category that my book *Evasion* is in on Kobo in Canada.

The book is listed in Mystery & Suspense / Thrillers as well as in Fiction & Literature / Thrillers.

Looking at the top-selling books in that category, here are the CAD price points I am seeing in the top-ten (the first page of results on a typical Kobo page top-seller list is twelve titles). It's best to drill down a bit more, but for the sake of simplicity, I'll stick with the top ten here:

$15.99, $3.99, $12.99, $3.99, $3.99, $0.99, $15.99, $2.99, $1.99, $3.99 CAD
Total = $669 CAD
Total divided by 10 = $6.69 CAD

This would suggest that a reasonable average price point for this category might be $6.99 CAD. I'll make a note of that as *Price Factor 1*.

Price Factor 2: Comparable Paperback Price

This factor is a bit more difficult, particularly if you don't have a paperback out or planned. But this is a factor book buyers likely consider.

Simply, I like to **START** by finding a price factor that is about 50% of what the paperback price for the same book is (or might be, if one existed).

And, while it's much easier to see the paperback comparison factor when shopping on Amazon, which shows print books and eBooks on the same item page, this *does* happen for plenty of Kobo's retail partners like Chapters/Indigo in Canada, or WHSmith in the UK.

Based on the size (and print costs) involved in the print/POD version, what would a reasonable price be. (Again, you might want to look at what similar sized/category titles in your genre are). But a typical trade paperback price in Canada is anywhere between $12.99 to $24.99 Canadian. $14.99 to $16.99 is right in the middle.

Considering my print costs for this book, which, when factoring in USD to CAD exchange plus shipping costs (there are no major scale POD operations like CreateSpace/KDP Print or Ingram Spark in Canada – all of it needs to be shipped across the border, which inflates those costs), my per unit print cost on Evasion is somewhere in the $6 CAD ballpark. I like to ensure more than a 50% markup from costs so that, when I offer the book through distribution channels, there's room for a generous discount to the bookseller (decades of being a bookseller helps me understand this in an intimate way), so a price of $14.99 would mean that a bookstore could buy the book for $7.49 at a 50% discount and I'd still earn about $1.50. The key is I wouldn't lose money.

Again, if you don't have a paperback, take a look at the top-selling titles in the print category for your book, or, perhaps, the print editions of the same books you spotted when looking at the eBook pricing.

You will, similarly, land on a range and average for paperback pricing.

In my case, I based it on my raw costs. Evasion is priced at $14.99.

Paperback Price: $14.99 CAD
50% of that price = $7.49 CAD

So now I have two price factors.

Price Factor One: $6.69 CAD
Price Factor Two: $7.49 CAD

This would suggest, finding the happy medium, a price of **$6.99**. (I'll get into the psychology of price later in this chapter). Now it is time to apply Price Factor Three.

Price Factor 3: Personal Price Factor

This is the easiest or perhaps the hardest factor to consider. It is your personal preference, your personal choice. It is a part of your larger author brand. It represents the intimately personal philosophy you hold as a writer, a creator and an artist struggling to align that with a business-minded approach. It butts heads with your ego, which, for most authors, involves a lack of ego, or at least lack of confidence. It struggles with your knowledge that the blood, sweat and tears you put into your book makes it virtually priceless. It struggles with the price that you, as a consumer and reader yourself, are willing to pay for an eBook.

Somewhere, in all that mess, confusion and in-depth reflection, is a price you honestly believe is a reasonable price for someone to pay for the work you have produced.

And that's how you adjust that price you landed on from comparing Price Factor One and Price Factor Two either up or down.

I landed on $6.99 CAD. But then I considered my *Personal Price Factor.*

Some of my raw and unedited thoughts that were involved, include:

- *Evasion* is a relatively shorter novel. 53,000 words
- I am a virtual unknown name as an author – who would dare take a chance on reading me? Why would they? (Again, remember, much of this voice is the self-deflating ego and "imposter syndrome" that authors constantly struggle with)
- I did put a lot of effort and heart into this book,
- I also paid for editing, for graphics to use for the cover, for formatting for the paperback version*
- I also spent a crapload of money (thousands) on the audiobook version that I would like to earn back one day*

* *Yes, I know that the paperback and audiobook version aren't related to the eBook, but as a business-minded author it's*

important to consider the overall investment and overall ways that the investment can be recouped.

Ultimately, I thought that $6.99 was a bit high for the length of the novel as well as for my lesser known presence/brand as a writer of thrillers.

So, I initially decided on $5.99 CAD.

It was a reasonable price. Not too high. Not too low.

It also allows me the opportunity and flexibility to do price discounts and promotions. Changing a book from $2.99 to $0.99 isn't much of a discount. It's $2.00. But changing it from $5.99 to $0.99 is a $5 discount; or changing it from $5.99 to $2.99 was a $3 discount, and a much more attractive deal.

So, I initially decided upon $5.99 CAD and $4.99 USD (based on basic exchange rates plus rounding, which I'll talk about in more detail later)

But then, with consideration for the Canadian consumer, who are often subject to insane and over-inflated USD to CAD conversions (the average mass market paperback that sells for $6.99 or $7.99 USD retails for between $9.99 and $12.99 CAD), part of my consumer-minded brain suggested I do something of benefit to Canadian readers.

So, I went with $4.99 USD and $4.99 CAD. I priced them at par.

It felt good.

I did this in complete recognition that I was leaving $1.00 per transaction on the table. But I was okay with that.

One last factor about *Evasion*'s pricing relates to the understanding that, once I get my act together and write the two follow-up books in the series meant to come after *Evasion,* I am either going to make *Evasion* FREE or offer it for $0.99 or $2.99 as a "funnel" book into that series.

This is just a single example of the process I went through, the deliberations I made, when I determined the price for one of my books. I'm not suggesting that this is the right process, nor the only one to use. It is simply one method, and a method that I usually work with. Your own process, your own *Personal Price Factor,* your own genre, category and process need to be something that works for you.

The key, and what I'm hoping you take away from this, is that your pricing should be deliberate, responsive and strategic.

The Basic Psychology of Price

We understand why products are priced at $0.99 instead of $1.00 — even though we all know better. Ninety-nine cents always feels like a better price that one dollar.

But why is that?

When consumers look at a price, they mentally round any price they see UP to the next dollar. So, when they see $1.00, they have already rounded up to $2.00 automatically. It happens almost subconsciously.

Thus, $0.99 feels like $1.00, whereas $1.00 feels more like $2.00.

It's a bit of a silly notion, but continued studies of customer price psychology demonstrate that is how our minds typically work.

Understanding and remember this becomes important once we start converting our prices into different currencies.

If you enter a price of $2.99 USD for your eBook, Kobo (and all the other major retailers) will use an automated price currency conversion to change the price to the local currency for different territories.

$2.99 USD might become $3.63 CAD (based on exchange rates typical in the summer of 2018 when I'm writing this)

Basic high school economics might tell you that as price increases, sales will decline. But remember, that, within certain price bands, there's that psychological factor in pricing.

When a consumer sees $3.63 CAD, they have already rounded up to $4.00 automatically in their mind.

Thus, manually over-writing the CAD price from $3.63 to $3.99, makes very little difference in a consumer's mind — and the extra margin you can make from rounding the prices up will more than make up for any drop in unit sales.

You might think that it's a mere $0.36. (Or, more realistically, 70% of $0.36, which is about $0.25)

But, with 100 copies sold, that difference is $25.

With 500 copies sold, that difference becomes $125.

With 1000 copies sold, that difference becomes $250.

And with 5000 copies sold, it's $1250.

Those pennies that you ignore can add up over time.

Isn't that extra change better in your pocket than left on the table?

Optimizing Prices in a Top-Selling Country

So how do you know what territories to optimize your price in and what territories to leave alone? Kobo Writing Life allows for optimization in 16 different currencies. That's a lot of work for a matter of pennies.

Considering your time and the energy spent on pricing strategies is also important; therefore, focusing on the territories where you are selling more might offer you the best return on your time investment.

As mentioned in the previous chapter and based on my own experience working with thousands of authors over the years, it was typical that anywhere from 60% to 75% of an author's Kobo sales would come from Canada and Australia.

So, what if that author enters a USD price and lets the systems do the auto-conversion to both USD and AUD?

Let's look at a book that is priced $3.99 USD using a May 2018 exchange rate for USD to CAD and AUD currencies.

In the chart below:

- ***Auto-CAD** and **Auto-AUD** reflect the automatically converted retail price*
- ***Earnings USD** represents the earnings converted back to USD prices for easy comparison*

- ***Manual CAD** and **Manual AUD** reflect manually controlled/adjusted prices*

	Price	Earnings per unit	Earnings USD
USD Price	$3.99	$2.79	$2.79
Auto-CAD	$5.18	$3.63	$2.79
Auto-AUD	$5.35	$3.75	$2.81
USD Price	$3.99	$2.79	$2.79
Manual CAD	$5.99	$4.19	$3.23
Manual AUD	$5.99	$4.19	$3.14

The difference, per unit, isn't all that much. If you manually tweak your pricing, you would earn:

- 44 cents more for each sale in Canada
- 33 cents more for each sale in Australia

But let's see what happens when we match these new prices to actual unit sales.

Say, for example, that you sell 100 books. Based on my study of Kobo author sales in the past five years, I'm going to say that 50% of those books will be sold in Canada, 25% in Australia, and 18% in the USA.

	Price	Earnings per unit	Earnings USD	Sales Volume	Total Earnings
USD Price	$3.99	$2.79	$2.79	18	$50.27
Auto-CAD	$5.18	$3.63	$2.79	50	$139.60
Auto-AUD	$5.35	$3.75	$2.81	25	$70.22
USD Price	$3.99	$2.79	$2.79	18	$50.27
Manual CAD	$5.99	$4.19	$3.23	50	$161.43
Manual AUD	$5.99	$4.19	$3.14	25	$78.62

Your earnings, in Canada, is suddenly almost $22 higher. In Australia, it's $9 higher. I'm not sure about you, but I'd rather have that $30 or so in my own pocket.

Considering the long-term effect on earnings. Sure, it's great to sell 100 copies of a book. But what does that extra income, become when it is 500 units or 1000 units?

Are you willing to leave that extra "change" on the table, particularly on a retailer like Kobo, where a higher volume of sales outside the US tends to be the norm?

Proven Pricing Strategies

One thing to remember, in addition to the psychology of the .99 price point is that a price that falls outside of the expected norm (in North America, for example, .99 looks like a "natural" price point, even though we know there's nothing natural about it). So, when you price in a price point that is typical or normal from the local consumers perspective, it looks like the book was custom-listed in that country/territory rather than an automated import.

It's deliberate.

As mentioned in the previous section (where I just looked at USD, CAD and AUD), no, you don't have to manually adjust and control your prices in every single one of the 16 prices that KWL allows you to control). But if you do, pay attention to *where* controlling those prices might have the best effect. In the example I previously used, I choose two territories where KWL authors typically see higher volumes. For you, it might be different. But, in a nutshell, and again, based on the most common currencies for overall sales, volume, it's likely you'll want to consider the following currencies for adjustments.

- **USD, CAD, AUD, NZD, GBP, EUR**

The following tips are derived from six years of analyzing pricing trends at Kobo and helping authors to optimize their prices. I have summarized them below based on a combination of customer psychology and an understanding of customer behavior as seen from a retailer's perspective on eBook sales in those territories.

USD Suggestions

- Use a .99 price point.
- Keep your price relatively low, since the majority of your sales are likely coming from Kindle, where bargain-hunters are still popular. And, given that your prices need to be consistent across retailers, being too aggressive on your USD pricing might negatively impact your KDP/Kindle sales.

CAD, AUD, NZD Suggestions

- Round the auto-converted price up to the nearest/next .99 (use "nearest" or "next" while keeping the consumer's perspective in mind. That could be the difference between a reasonable price adjustment or a rip-off).
- Slightly higher price tolerance:
  - Keep in mind that consumers in CAD, AUD and NZD are often "ripped off" when it comes to USD to CAD, AUD and NZD converted book prices. This happens in both print and eBooks. So, the tolerance, in consumers is for inflated pricing. You can leverage that by pricing a little bit more aggressively higher, while considering a "value" or good deal for the consumer.
    - For example, if a book is priced at $6.99 USD, then the CAD price might be $9.11. In this case, I'd be tempted to round down to $8.99, or, perhaps, even $7.99 CAD. I might do the same thing for AUD and NZD, where the currency conversion is typically similar to the USD to CAD conversion rates.

GBP (UK) Suggestions

- Round auto-converted price down to the nearest .49 or .99. (The reason for this because since GBP is a stronger currency (numerically speaking), .49 is almost as common as .99 to consumers)

- The second reason for rounding DOWN in GBP by default, rather than nearest is because most of the larger publishers in the UK are typically pricing low as an overall strategy. So the idea of being an indie author and coming in slightly below the market average means being a bit more aggressive with lower prices in the UK

EUR Suggestions

- Round to the nearest .49 or .99. (The reasoning here is related to the relative strength of the Euro, which is similar to the GBP mentioned above)
- Unlike in GBP for the UK, rounding to the nearest rather than defaulting to rounding down works well. There are many European countries, such as France, where there are significant "price protection" controls in the book market (implemented as measures of preservation of culture and art) and where Amazon's pricing scheme doesn't control the market. Consumers buy based on their perceived value for creative works rather than "scavenging the bargain bin." So consider a reasonable consumer-friendly, but not-author bleeding type price.

Kobo Writing Life's Price Scheduling Tool

One of the best tools for marketing for authors are taking advantage of the third-party eBook promotion platforms that come in the way of direct to consumer mailing lists, such as BookBub or BargainBooksy and many others.

The basis behind these platforms is that customers sign up to receive notifications, usually through email about discounted or free books within a category they enjoy reading and specific to a platform (Kindle, Kobo, iBooks, Nook, etc.) that they prefer to read on.

Authors submit their titles (usually with an expectation that the eBook will be temporarily discounted from the regular price to either free or usually something between $0.99 and $2.99), the submissions are vetted, and, if they are accepted, the author pays, the promotion is scheduled, and then the author ensures to make the price change on the appropriate day, waits for the email blast from that third-party platform to go out, then they watch their sales increase.

For most authors, BookBub is the Holy Grail of these platforms. As David Gaughran infamously said at the *Smarter Artist Summit* in 2017 in response to a question about BookBub: "What's BookBub? It's a site that makes money rain on your face."

BookBub, of course, isn't the only platform like this. There are hundreds. And they can work nicely for getting more traction for your sales on Kobo, Kindle and the other retailers. I talk, more, of course, about Kobo's built-in PROMOTIONS tab later on in this book, so I don't want to get ahead of myself.

Let's just say that running temporary price promotions is something that works for growing sales and your reader base.

But sales promotions usually require you having to make a note in your calendar to log onto the platforms to make the updates, ideally, not too long before midnight the day before your promo begins. Then remembering, after the promotion is over, to go and change it back to the regular price.

If you have ever been exclusive to Amazon Kindle via KDP Select, then you may be familiar with one of the tools they only give authors who are exclusive. During the 90 Day exclusivity period, KDP offers limited opportunities to schedule FREE or discount (KINDLE COUNTDOWN DEAL) promotions.

Kobo Writing Life, however, doesn't ask for exclusivity and offers this option to their authors as often as they want to take advantage of it.

Which means you can schedule a price change months in advance and not have to be logged into your dashboard at midnight the day before the promo with a finger hovering over the "submit" button.

KWL offers the ability for authors to set up and schedule either permanent price changes or temporary price changes using a handy built-in price-scheduling tool.

In the chapter ***Navigating the Basics of Kobo Writing Life*** sub-section *Set the Price* we looked at the price controls. But for your convenience (particularly if you skipped that chapter, and, even if you didn't, it never hurts to be reminded of a convenient tool) below are the basic steps you can take to make changes to your price.

The first thing to remember is that there are two types of price changes you can make. You can **Schedule a sale** or **Schedule a price change**.

- **Schedule a sale** is used for a temporary price change; one that has a start and an end date. For example, you want your book to be priced down to $0.99 for the duration of a day, a week, a month or some other period that you determine, but, at the end of that period, the price goes back to the regular price

- **Schedule a price change** is used if you want to change the price but to schedule that change at some future date. For example, let's say you are offering your book, while it is in pre-order, for a special low "pre-order" price in order to entice people to order it early and help you climb the best-seller/ranking charts. You might schedule a price change for your book for the day after launch day back to the regular price.

To schedule a sale, go to the EBOOKS tab of the book you want to edit and then click on the **Set the price** tab along the right-hand side.

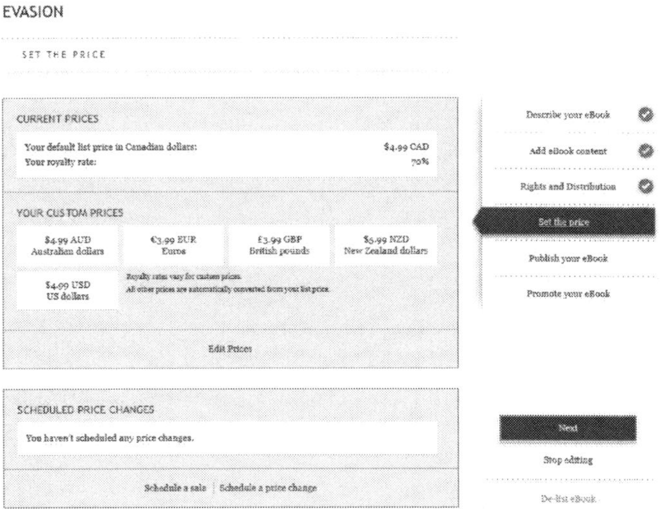

Click on **Schedule a sale**. In the pop-up window that appears, select the start and end date for this sale. Then, add any of the currencies that you want to modify during the sale, along with the corresponding price in that currency.

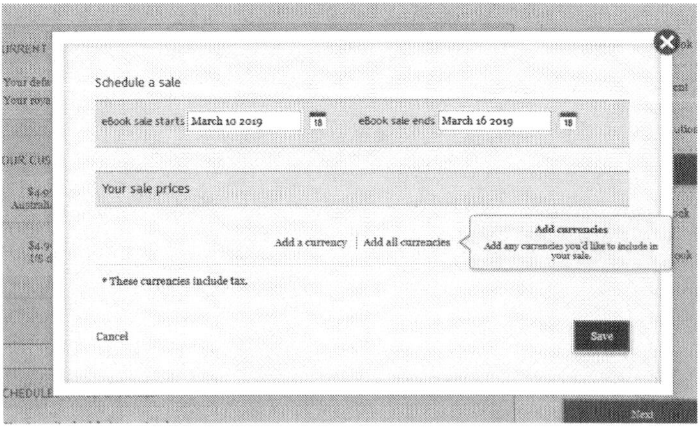

(Yes, you can schedule a price to only change in a particular currency, such as only in USD, and leave your prices in CAD, GBP, AUD and other manually adjusted prices regular price).

In the example below, you'll see I scheduled a price change to $0.99 from March 10, 2019 to March 16, 2019 in USD, CAD, GBP, AUD, NZD and EUR.

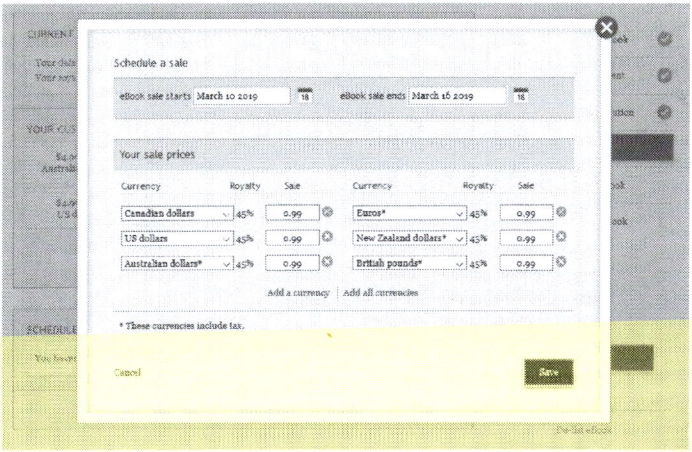

When you are done making the price edits you desire, click on **SAVE**.

You will then see, in the **Set the price** screen, the fact that you have scheduled a price change during a particular time period. If you click on **Edit** on the *Book goes on sale* line, you'll be able to see and adjust your price. You also have the option to **Cancel** the sale. If you want to **Edit** the prices of your regular eBook price for when the sale is over (ie, different than your current prices), click on **Edit** on the *Regular price resumes* line.

Scheduling a price change allows the same flexibility of currency and prices (for example, if you plan on only permanently changing a price in a single currency), but in this particular case, there is no end date, just the date the price changes.

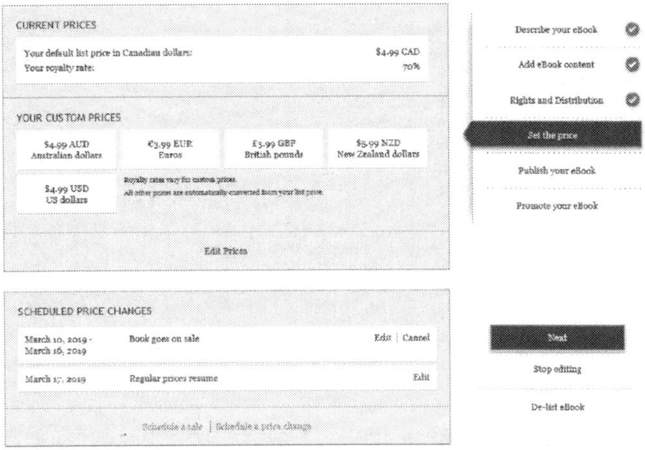

In the next chapter, ***Taking Full Advantage of the "NO CAP" on 70% Royalties,*** we'll get into a different type of price optimization.

But in the meantime, amidst all the pricing gymnastics, screen shots, basic math and examples we just walked through, don't forget the fact that price is a verb, not a noun, and that experimenting with, testing, and being flexible to understand how price operates different in different currencies and culture, is important to your path to success.

It is far from a "set-it-and-forget-it" type of thing.

TAKING FULL ADVANTAGE OF THE "NO CAP" ON 70% ROYALTIES

IN THE CHAPTER on ***Price Optimization***, we looked at ways to maximize the margin per unit sale by paying attention to global currencies, sales trends and customer psychology. But there's an often-over-looked way that authors can leverage high earnings potential at Kobo.

In this chapter we'll examine how authors have been able to take full advantage of the fact there is no cap on the 70% royalty earning for Kobo sales.

Kindle's $2.99 to $9.99 Price Window

Most authors are familiar with the $2.99-$9.99 USD price window that Amazon's Kindle Direct Publishing has established. If a book is priced within that window, an author can earn 70% for each unit sale (*minus a small mostly hidden delivery fee based on the eBook's file size*). If a book is priced lower than $2.99 or higher than $9.99, KDP pays them 35% per unit sale.

Kindle also has certain territories (India, Japan, Brazil and Mexico) where you will earn 35% regardless of price unless your eBook is exclusive to Kindle by opting in to KDP Select.

But there's no such price cap at Kobo.

Let me repeat that because I believe it bears repeating and fully appreciating.

There is no price cap at Kobo.

If you price beyond $9.99 on Kobo, you still earn the full 70%.

Why?

Because there is no price cap at Kobo.

I know it seems repetitious, but sometimes we need to hear something multiple times before it takes a hold.

Here is another small thing that most authors might not be aware of, or perhaps not fully appreciate.

If you price lower than $2.99 on Kobo, you earn 45%. The lowest actual price you can set on Kobo is $0.99. There is no $0.01 to $0.98 (unless it lands in that area based on automated currency conversion). You can make the book FREE (which we'll talk about in the next chapter), but the lowest price you can actually set is $0.99.

So, if your price is below $2.99, you earn 45%, which is 10% higher than the standard terms offered at Kindle Direct Publishing.

Ten percent might not seem like much of a big deal. But, remember how, in the last chapter we looked at the way that pennies could add up once the volume of sales increased? That same thing works here.

A book that sells at $1.99 earns $0.70 at 35%.

But at 45%, that same book earns $0.90.

That is a $0.20 difference.

The twenty-cent difference might not mean much for a handful of sales. But let's pretend that book is a moderate seller and sells a single copy a day.

At 35% it would earn $255.50 in a year.

At 45% it would earn $328.50 in a year.

An additional $73 in your pocket based on moderate sales.

I'd take it.

But let's go back to the higher end of the price spectrum, which tends to be a place that most indie authors avoid.

The concept of selling eBooks for more than $10 doesn't sound much like competitive pricing. Perhaps for a single book it's not all that competitive, particularly when compared to the average price point of an eBook from one of the big five publishers. But, as you'll see below, there are definitely some cases in which you'll want to price yourself well above that ten-dollar threshold.

Kobo Customers and Price Sensitivity

In 2011, John Locke, an American author from Kentucky, became the first self-published author to sell more than a million eBooks on Amazon by pricing his "Donovan Creed" novels at 99 cents.

As expected, that captured a lot of attention.

And it also set a huge trend in indie publishing that continues to be debated to this day.

Most indie authors consistently price their books well below the industry average.

Part of the reason is confidence. There is a "the reader might take a chance on a lesser known writer like me if the price is really low" factor. Part of the reason is plain old undercutting in the price between a self-published author's title and a comparable traditionally published book. "You can buy two or more of my eBooks for the same price as a single eBook from one of the big five publishers."

Kindle customers have repeatedly been conditioned to shop in the "bargain bin" at the front of the store. Some customers have even decried that they would never pay more than five dollars for a full-length book.

However, Kobo customers aren't as conditioned as Kindle customers have been to look for bargain-priced reads. Part of the reason might stem from something we saw when we looked at the global nature of Kobo. Given Kobo's origins and popularity in Canada as well as in other territories like Australia, where the price of print books can be ridiculously high, a slightly higher eBook price, by comparison, still presents as a decent value.

This doesn't mean that Kobo customers don't enjoy a good deal, a sale or want to take advantage of a great promotional offer. But it means that your $6.99 CAD priced eBook is still anywhere from 40% to 60% cheaper than a comparable title from a big publisher.

As you can see illustrated in the *Kobo Volume 2017 by Price Point* chart, there are some amazing opportunities for authors to move their pricing out of the $0.99 to $2.99 bargain-bin ghetto and explore slightly higher pricing to maximize their revenue.

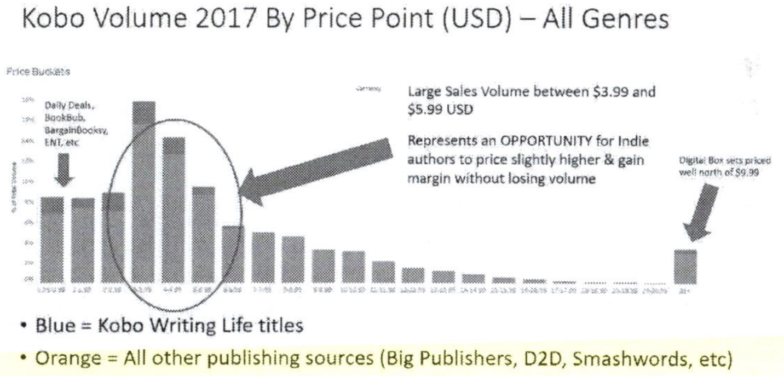

Let me pause to provide a cautionary note here to clarify what I am suggesting, because I have seen this type of statement misinterpreted many times.

I am **not** suggesting that you over-price your books on Kobo, nor that you "rip-off" customers in territories like Canada, Australia and New Zealand. I am merely pointing out the trends; in those territories, the price of books is already significantly inflated. So the price tolerance in consumers is higher.

And that represents an opportunity.

The tolerance comes from the history of bookselling in places like Canada and Australia. There are multiple economic factors at play, such as the size of the economies, the cost of shipping across the border, the licensing of rights. It costs money to put books on a boat and to ship them around the world, or to warehouse them across a border. However, those costs don't exist with digital books. And yet the majority of the larger publishers still follow the same pricing structure for their eBooks.

Which means that you can price your eBooks in those markets slightly higher while still offering customers a reprieve from the inflated and often outrageous pricing that is seen coming from major international publishers who seem more interested in driving customers back to buying dead trees they are shipping around the world rather than eBooks.

Using the "No Cap" To Your Advantage

One of the most common strategies successful authors use is writing books in a series, or, if not a series, writing multiple books. When you have enough titles in a series, or enough books in your backlist, a great way to increase earnings while giving your readers a deal is offering up a digital box set of titles.

Let's imagine you have 3 eBooks that sell individually for $3.99 USD. If a customer were to buy each book individually, it would cost them a total of $11.97 and you would earn $8.38. But to appeal to the customer's desire to get a bargain, you can put those books into a 3-eBook digital bundle, or boxset for those books and price it at $9.99.

This saves the customer about three dollars and helps you earn 70% of $9.99 (which would be $6.99) in a single sale TODAY, rather than a potentially higher amount of money over time selling all 3 eBooks individually.

But what happens when you have more books, or if your eBooks were priced higher?

Let's say each book was $4.99 individually.

That would make the total $14.97 for all three. Setting a price of $9.99 saves the customer about five dollars and you earn $9.99.

And, if you price the book at $10.99, on Amazon your royalties drop to 35%, turning your earnings to $3.85. It is still a great deal for the customer, but it immediately cuts your margin from each sale in half.

However, on Kobo, you can earn 70% of that larger number.

Which means that bundling higher priced books, or more books into a single digital box set creates a new world of possibilities.

Romance author Lauren Royal was the first author to break into this strategy on Kobo in a major way in 2015.

In an interview on the Kobo Writing Life Blog in a September 21, 2015 article entitled "How my $19.99 Boxed Set Became a #1 Kobo Bestseller," Lauren explained her reasoning behind doing this. "I felt I'd gone too long between releases, but I had nothing brand-new in the works that would be ready for release soon."

All of her full-length books had already been in 3-book box sets that had been selling really well for her. So she wondered what might happen if she merged two box sets together and also added in a few shorter bonus titles in order to sweeten the deal.

That is how her "Complete Chase Family Series" digital box set was born. She priced it at $19.99, and her only additional costs were the price of a new cover and the time to format the new book.

Her $19.99 box set of 8 titles, which was a great value to her readers, hit #1 on the overall best-seller list on Kobo. It wasn't only the top-selling book on Kobo (outselling one of that year's biggest hits, *Fifty Shades of Grey* sequel *Grey*), but she also earned $14 per unit sale.

Lauren also submitted the eBook to several promotions. It appeared in a cheekily named landing page titled "Can't Get It On Kindle," had been in a 30% off feature (internal Kobo promotions are something we'll look at in more detail in a later chapter), which helped move a decent number of units, but the tipping point came when the book, which had already started to trend, caught a merchandiser's eye and ended up being hand-selected to be featured in the top of "read the entire series" email blast to Kobo customers at its regular full price of $19.99.

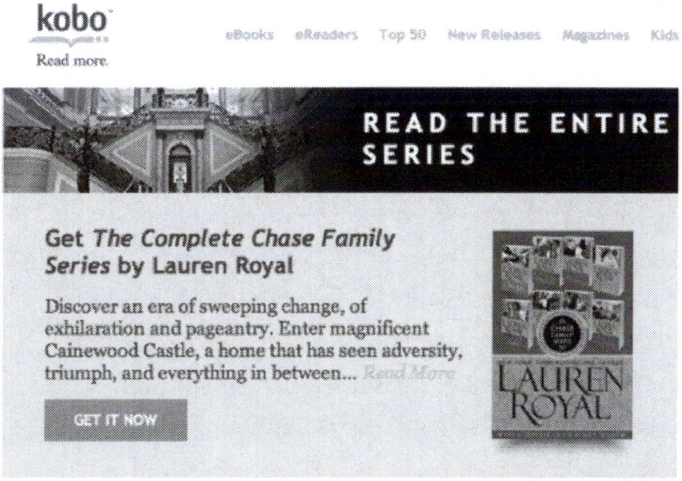

I'm sure you can imagine that earning $14 per unit sale and selling enough to be the number one book on Kobo is an extremely more profitable venture than selling even 10 times as many books priced at 99 cents and only earning 35 cents per sale.

Let's say that Lauren sold 500 copies of that book in a single day to hit that best-seller stat.

(I'm completely making that number up, by the way. I can't remember her actual unit sales, and, even if I did remember, that information is confidential and isn't something I would share).

At 500 unit sales she would earn $7,000.

She would need to sell 20,000 units at $0.99 to earn the same amount.

The Best Way to Exploit These Better Terms Without Hurting Your Kindle Sales

As we looked at in the example from Lauren Royal, higher prices for digital box sets priced above $10.99 can be a killer move on Kobo.

But it doesn't work all that well on Kindle.

What if you have 8 titles, all priced at $4.99? The combined cost would be close to $40. Even a value box set at $29.99 would earn only $10.49 on Kindle. But on Kobo a single unit sale would earn $20.99, which is twice as much.

It's great to earn so much on Kobo. But you'd be bleeding margin on Amazon.

The solution to that is simple.

Don't set up that larger box set on Kindle.

Your Kindle readers would still have access to the smaller box sets or the individual titles, so it's not a true exclusivity thing.

It's just an additional deal, or an additional offer, for your Kobo readers.

This type of creation is also something you can potentially use not just to appeal to your loyal readers on Kobo, but also to appeal to the humans at Kobo.

Having a value-based title that is available on Kobo and not available on any other platform can be appealing to them and might be worthy of spotlighting. That is where the landing page "Can't Get It On Kindle" originally came from. We'll look at that more in the chapter on catching a Kobo merchandiser's eye.

It should be noted that Apple Books (formerly iBooks), also doesn't have a cap on 70% earnings either, but if you create a box set or higher-priced item that doesn't appear on any other retailer and you email the team at Kobo Writing Life to let them know about it, they might be able to spotlight that has an "exclusive for Kobo readers only" title.

So don't forget to leverage this information both for your Kobo sales as well as sales at other platforms, like Apple Books.

Okay, so in this chapter and the previous one, we talked about optimizing price for maximum return and margin. But there are also ways that no price, or leveraging free can actually help you sell more and gain new readers on Kobo.

The next chapter, ***The Power of Free*** explores that in detail.

THE POWER OF FREE

FREE IS A strategy that many authors used to catapult their books into the stratosphere during the "Kindle Gold Rush" (about 2010 to 2012) era. Back in those days, the method was to make a book free, watch the book's downloads start to roll in, the ranking reach new heights (usually within the top 10 of its category), then flipping the book back to a paid status and riding that elevated rank as the free downloads converted into sales.

When Amazon changed the way they treated and ranked free titles, the "magic bullet" of using free went away. This happened about nearly the same time that they introduced KDP Select, their exclusivity program, the Kindle Unlimited "all you can read" program and limited an author's ability to make a book free for more than 5 days in a single 90-day exclusivity period.

You are likely to hear many authors bemoan this while stating that "free doesn't work any longer." If you listen a bit more intently, however, you are likely to also hear from others that free still works quite nicely, particularly on Kobo as well as on Apple Books.

The Most Searched Term at Kobo

This is something I regularly publicly shared when I was working at Kobo, based on statistics that the "Big Data" and web teams provided.

The most searched term at Kobo is "free."

The second most searched term at Kobo is "free books."

Followed by "free eBooks."

And the next most popular searches, most of the top 10 searches at any given time, is the word "free" along with some genre, such as "free romance," "free mystery," "free fiction," etcetera.

Because of this, and as a way to help KWL authors who were using free to expand their reader base and their sales at Kobo, I requested that, instead of having those searches go to a generic search results page that most likely showed tens of thousands of the same public domain titles over and over, that the Big Data team re-direct those searches to the localized version of a "Free" landing page that is curated and maintained by the KWL team.

Go ahead, go to www.kobo.com and type the word "free" into the search box.

Chances are that it'll land you on the localized version of the page:

https://www.kobo.com/free-ebooks

I talk a bit more about localization in the OTHER DETAILS AND HACKS chapter later in this book, but just know that if you are in the US, that link above will likely take you to a URL that looks like this:

https://www.kobo.com/us/en/p/free-ebooks

And if you are in Canada (like I am), it will take you here:

https://www.kobo.com/ca/en/p/free-ebooks

One thing to note is that, like Amazon, Kobo regularly changes the way things work and is constantly doing A/B testing, so some readers might find the site working the way I describe, while others might get a different result. These A/B tests are run to determine success for converting browsers into buyers and smart companies use that data to update and implement changes. This is how I convinced the Big Data team to implement the re-direct to the KWL-curated KWL landing page in the first place.

I mention that this landing page is curated by the Kobo Writing Life team, but there are a few dynamic elements to it.

The very top carousel *Today's Top Free eBooks* is a dynamically generated list that is updated multiple times per day and may be unique to the territory you are viewing it from.

But the rest of the page (with the exception, perhaps, of spots that the main merchandising team might submit titles into), is maintained by the KWL team.

This is due to legacy "traditional publishing" thinking that discounts and ignores the power and value of free. Something, of course, that the indie author community has more fully embraced.

The rest of the page, which features "hero" spots such as *Romance Editor's Pick* or regular carousels that show 6 titles at a time, such as *Mystery & Thriller*, is updated manually by a human at some time every Monday. Or, on long weekends where Monday is a holiday, it happens on the Tuesday.

The chapter entitled ***The Kobo Writing Life Promotions Tool*** goes into how that curation works in more detail.

Tracking Free at Kobo

If you publish your book to Kobo via a third-party aggregator such as Draft2Digital or Smashwords, the tracking of free downloads has constantly been reported in a relatively consistent fashion over the years.

The internal KWL free-tracking has, historically, been problematic. I won't get into the nitty-gritty behind-the-scenes reasons, other than to say that the KWL dashboard was originally built looking at a particular "bucket" of information that stores sales data, and that free downloads were recorded in a completely different series of other "buckets" that were a lot more difficult for the KWL dashboard to accurately capture.

But, after many iterations and updates, in December of 2017, the KWL dashboard was finally updated to include free tracking on the KWL Global map, and, using a little toggle switch on the dashboard, authors can easily see where and how many free copies of their eBooks are being downloaded.

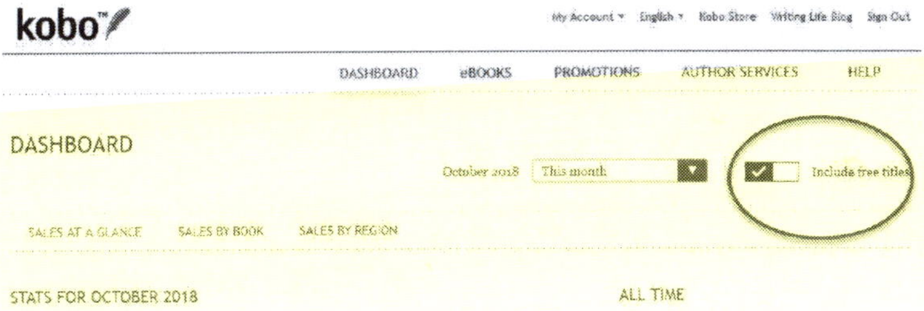

While the toggle doesn't allow you to see only free, it is still valuable to look at and better analyse how free is working (or not working) in your strategies.

And, you can select a single title that might have always been free to parse that out.

For example, if I look at my mini story collection ***Night Cries (Nocturnal Screams, Volume 1)*** which has been free on Kobo since I first published it there, I can see that, since May 2018 when I first released it on Kobo, the book has been downloaded in 45 different countries.

With a quick view of the map (without having to even get into doing the math), I can easily see that the most popular countries for free downloads are Canada, the United States, the UK, Australia and South Africa.

I can then look at book two in that series to see how those downloads are converting to sales in the same countries.

What Are the Best Free Strategies at Kobo?

There's more than one way to use Free to sell more at Kobo. And don't worry, even if you are nervous or hesitant about the use of free, you should know that there are multiple ways of using free strategically on Kobo; some of which don't even require you to price the book at $0.00.

I'll start with the most popular and successful strategies for free, but I will also explore the different methods and how they can benefit authors. Some of the features and strategies are unique to Kobo, and some are just generic best practices.

First Free in Series

Because you can set any book to $0.00 (Free) at any time for as long as you like at Kobo, without any requests for exclusivity, many authors who write series books will make the first book in their series free.

The concept is creating a funnel of a large volume of people to pick up and try the first book, and, if they read and enjoy the book, the characters, or the universe, they might perhaps convert into buyers of the next book in that series.

And there-in lies the rub.

If they read the first book.

Because, after performing and then sharing the results of repeated studies over the years via the KWL blog and at writers' conferences around the world, I found a very consistent pattern.

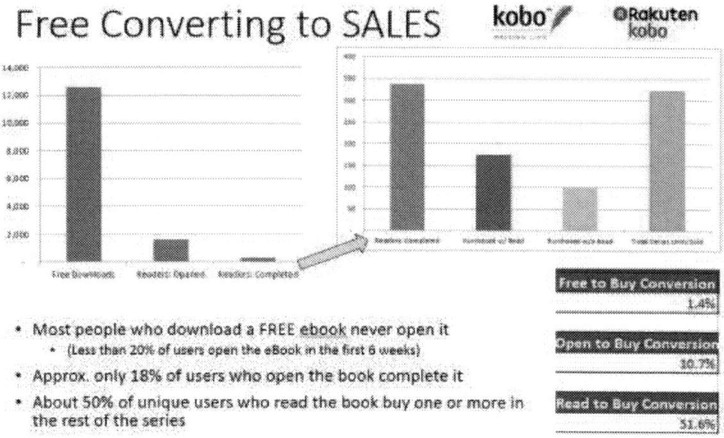

The *Free Converting to SALES* image is from a slide shared dozens of times in presentations and which appears publicly on the KWL Blog at www.kobowritinglife.com.

The slide is based on one specific study, but it matches a very consistent pattern that we saw for many other series promotions that had been tracked.

This specific slide shows a 6-book series where the first book was permanently free. Analysis was done on the action taken over a six-week period following when the book was first put onto a free promotion at Kobo.

The slide shows that most people who downloaded that free first in series eBook (about 12,000 people) never opened it.

So if you compare the download to sales conversion, or the "Free to Buy" conversion, you'll find a typical conversion rate of about 1.4%.

That is pretty standard.

But when we look in a little more detail, we determine that less than 2,000 of those 12,000 people actually opened the book.

That changes the conversion, because the "Open to Buy" conversion is a better number at 10.7%.

If you dig deeper, to look at the number of those 2,000 people who completed reading the book in that same six-week period, you'll see that less than 350 of them actually finished it. This means about 18% of users who opened the book completed it.

And the "Read to Buy" conversion is much more appealing at 51.6%.

There are additional stats that include a bit of mixed consumer behavior. Some customers bought 1 book in the series, while others bought all the rest of the books. Some customers even bought the other books before even opening or reading the free book one.

This skews the overall stats and makes it appear that the conversion of "Read to Buy" is closer to 100%.

The assumption is that, some customers might have been so intrigued by that first free book that they just bought the entire series immediately so that they could binge read it.

But it does lead to a few intriguing conclusions.

First, that you can earn revenue and convert free downloads into sales with a series.

Second, that the real trick isn't just getting them to download the book. The real strategy is getting them to open and complete that book.

If you can do that, you've got a winning strategy.

It Doesn't Have to Be the First Book in a Series

If you don't have a long series of books or are not comfortable with making a full book permanently free (and I'm not going to blame you – you likely put a great deal of blood, sweat, and tears into your book, not to mention the cost for things such as editing and cover design), you can create shorter related works or interstitial works that provide the same sort of funnel.

Perhaps it is a prequel short story. Or a novella that takes place between books one and two that features either a secondary character or an event that is only eluded to in the main novels.

Kobo supports *Series Title* metadata that uses decimals, so your prequel could be entered as volume 0. Or your interstitial novella could be entered as 1.5.

Heck, if you wanted to write 9 short stories that take places between books 1 and 2, you could release them using 1.1, 1.2, 1.3 . . . all the way through to 1.9.

The chart below, from a 2013 study, shows a "related title" for a series and how a promotion on that free book resulted in a significant increase in the sales of the related series book. (Note that the FREE and PAID titles are on different scales – the FREE numbers were significantly higher than the PAID ones, but they were placed together in order to illustrate the effect this promotion had.)

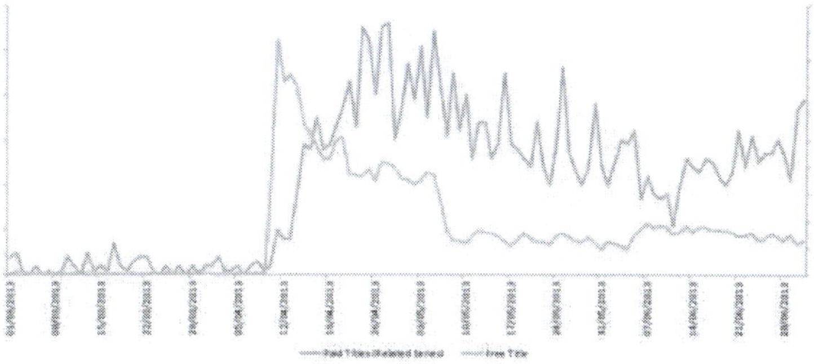

It Doesn't Have to Be Fiction

While the examples above are for fiction, the use of Free or the use of the ability to enter a "0" or decimal for a series isn't restricted to fiction.

Non-fiction authors who write in a series can employ a similar method.

Take, for example, the Fall 2018 release *Skeletons in my Closet: Life Lessons from a Homicide Detective* by Dave Sweet and Sarah Graham.

The full book is the first, and of the writing of this chapter, the only existing one in their *Unconventional Classroom* series. But, as part of a pre-release strategy and a way to offer the fans who had been waiting a long time for the book's release a little bit of a treat, the authors compiled a special digital chapbook of about 11,000 words entitled *Behind the Scenes: Skeletons in my Closet* and marked it as Volume 0 in the *Unconventional Classroom* series.

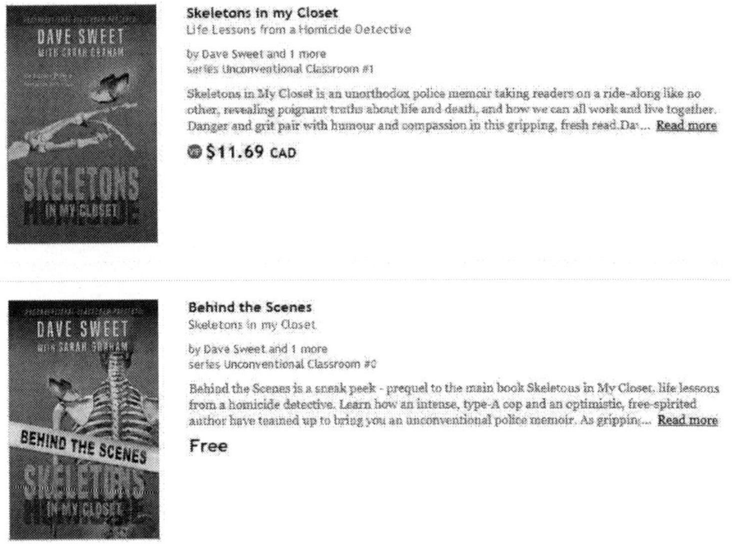

It also functions as a "funnel" that can hook more readers and ideally intrigue them into buying the full book.

It Doesn't Have to Be a Series

While conversion from Free to sales does seem to work best for books in a series, there are plenty of authors who write stand-alone books and who still use free with a similar "funnel" process in mind.

The key isn't the immediate hook of readers being enticed by the characters or the universe of a series, but the author themselves.

My good friend Sean Costello has (as of the writing of this chapter in the summer of 2018) yet to write anything other than stand alone thriller and horror novels.

And yet, he has been able to use free to entice new readers to want to read his other books.

His stand-alone thriller *Squall* for example, has well over 1000 reviews averaging 4 stars on Kobo, and plenty of the reviews include the following comments:

- *"This is the first book I've read by Sean Costello and it's great! I recommend it to anyone. I can't wait to read his other books!"*
- *"I really looked forward to reading Squall because it was the first book I read of Mr. Costello's . . . I promptly bought the other six ebooks Mr. Costello wrote and look forward to reading them too."*
- *". . . a nice quick read and will probably read others from this author."*
- *"Quite a good thriller. Would recommend. Will read more of Sean Costello."*
- *"First time reading this author but not the last."*

I could keep going, because there are well over 1000 reviews on Kobo (and about 4,000 on Amazon), but I think you likely get the point: people read the perma-free title from Sean and then are enticed by his writing, to read the other stand-alone books he has written.

It Doesn't Have to Be a Full Book

In the example about non-fiction above, I shared the 11,000 word "Behind the Scenes" eBook that Dave Sweet and Sarah Graham used as a free "funnel" book into the first book in their non-fiction series.

I just wanted to point out, or remind you if you already noticed, that the free thing you offer doesn't need to be a full book.

I've done this plenty of times.

I have a 10,000 short story called "This Time Around" which was the genesis for my novel *A Canadian Werewolf in New York*. The story was originally meant to be a single stand-alone tale outlining how one man with the werewolf curse deals with a typical morning of waking up naked miles from home and no memory of the night before. After reading the story, my good friend Sean Costello said. "That's good. But I want to know what happens next." He kept pressing me to fill out the details of the rest of my main character's day, and the novel was born. *This Time Around* is now considered volume 0 in the "Canadian Werewolf" series and is a lead-gen title into that universe.

I've done similar perma-free shorter eBooks as ways for people to sample my other books which aren't part of a series.

Snowman Shivers is a permanently free two-story digital chapbook that contains two stories from my very first book, a short story collection, *One Hand Screaming*.

And *Prospero's Ghost* is a free short story that I co-wrote with Kimberly Foottit that is meant to be a sampler for the full-length anthology *Campus Chills* which I edited.

What If You're Not Comfortable with Free

Even if you aren't comfortable with making a book or even a shorter work free or permanently free, there are other ways that "free" can work for you at Kobo.

Previews

At Kobo, customers have the option to read the first 5% of any eBook in the catalog. This allows them the experience of being able to sample from a book before they buy it.

The way that previews work at Kobo is when an ePub file is ingested, an automated process runs in the background that grabs the first 5% of the book that tacks on a final page with a "BUY NOW" button.

When browsing online, customers have two ways they can preview a book. They can preview the book in a pop-up window, or they can save the aforementioned preview ePub file into their reader library.

As you can see in the screen shot of Adam Croft's *In the Name of the Father*, there is a "Preview Now" and a "Save Preview" option.

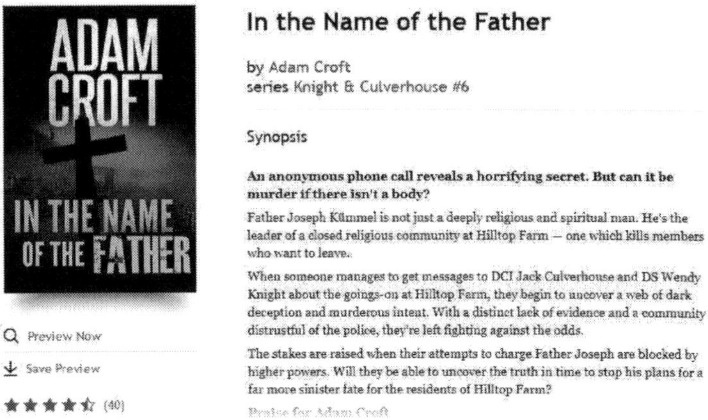

Regardless of which one you choose, the end of that preview sample will show you the "BUY NOW" screen.

Studies of customer behavior have revealed that as many as 50% of the customers who actually read through to the end of the 5% of the free preview of a book end up clicking on the "BUY NOW" button.

Because Kobo automates the free preview based on the first 5% of the content of the ePub file, (Alternatively, Apple Books allows for the manual creation of a unique and carefully crafted preview file), in order to optimize this, you might consider slightly altering the "front matter" of your book to ensure that the first 5% preview isn't just the prefatory table of contents, dedication and similar matter, but that the potential reader can actually begin to "sink their teeth" into the start of the main content of the book.

OverDrive (Library)

Libraries create an amazing opportunity for discoverability of new reading that is free for library patrons.

Getting your eBook into a global library system via OverDrive is easy with Kobo either directly through Kobo Writing Life, or through a third-party aggregator like Draft2Digital.

In either case, this is another way of using free to gain new readers and to also earn a little additional revenue.

I talk about Kobo and OverDrive in more detail in the chapter *Additional Revenue Opportunities Via Kobo.*

Kobo Plus

With their retail partner BOL.com in the Netherlands

(and Belgium), Kobo launched an "all you can read" eBook subscription service called *Kobo Plus*.

And, unlike Amazon's Kindle Unlimited program, there is no exclusivity requirement. Any indie author can opt their titles in to *Kobo Plus* either through Kobo Writing Life or via a third-party distributor like Draft2Digital.

This allows Kobo and BOL.com customers in NL and BE to read your book for free, increasing your discoverability on Kobo and earning you additional revenue.

I discuss this in further detail, including how to opt your titles into this program in the chapter *Additional Revenue Opportunities Via Kobo.*

CATCHING A KOBO MERCHANDISER'S EYE

IN THE CHAPTER ***The Humans Behind Kobo and Kobo Writing Life*** I wrote about the people behind the scenes. In this chapter I focus very specifically on the merchandisers at Kobo and how that differs from the Kindle store.

Countless books, blog posts, articles and podcasts feature ways that authors can leverage the ever-changing Amazon algorithms to increase their Kindle sales. So, even though there are similar automated processes that work at Kobo, this retailer places a significant emphasis on manual human curation and merchandising.

What is Merchandising?

Merchandising is the activity of promoting the sale of goods and usually refers to the process by which those products are displayed in a retail space.

It is a term that is regularly used in physical retail in relation to the layout of a store where shelves, aisles and end-caps are specifically designated for specific products or seasonal promotions.

Chain stores, for example, may designate very detailed and prescribed ways that certain products and brands are to be displayed for specific periods of time.

If you walk into a Barnes and Noble (US), a Chapters/Indigo (Canada) or a WHSmith (UK) for example, the end cap displays, and table displays and even some of the highlighted new releases are very likely based on a carefully curated merchandising plan created in each company's home office and deployed to stores.

Many of these spots are also co-op or paid-for spaces where publishers and sales agencies have invested significant dollars into ensuring that those products are given prime real estate across the chain.

The same holds true for most physical retailers, grocery stores, etc.

How Does Merchandising Work at Kobo?

Because Kobo was born out of a physical retailer (Indigo Books and Music, Inc), they follow similar plans to that of a traditional bookstore. Almost everything you see when you visit the Kobo website is based on a merchandising plan or strategy that has been carefully planned out weeks and months in advance.

Of course, instead of aisles, there are landing pages, features and browse categories where these products are slotted.

The "front window" of the storefront, and around 20 to 50 other landing pages that the storefront leads to, is managed by a team of human merchandisers.

Each landing page or feature page is likely some sort of a combination of "manually" placed titles, or systematically generated lists based on top-sellers within a category or a curated subset of eBooks.

Unlike in a physical bookstore, the eBook merchandiser isn't limited by the delivery of physical stock and also has access to detailed in-depth analytical data that helps them continue to revise and optimize sales conversion and also control dynamic updates based on customer activity.

For example, a carousel of hot new releases in a genre might be a list of 100 titles that the merchandiser felt were relevant, but the list itself may be sorted so that the titles selling the highest volume appear closer to the top of that list.

Merchandising at Kobo is Global

Kobo has more than a dozen versions of their online store in different global territories, and many of them are each managed by separate merchandisers. The look and feel of the stores in Canada, Italy, Brazil, Australia, Spain, and the Netherlands, for example, are all designed with readers in each of those countries in mind.

The best way to understand the differences is by viewing how each country's storefront and the localized bestseller lists look by checking out the Global view on Kobo for yourself.

In the ***Price Optimization*** chapter under *Seeing How Your Price Looks in Other Countries* I explained how you can see the way the different Kobo storefronts appear in various regions around the world.

You can use this not just to look at pricing, but to get a feel for the way that different titles and features are displayed on Kobo. There are seasonal and cultural differences. Erotica titles aren't visible in Turkey, for example. Seasonal features like "hot beach reads" will be different for North America and Australia. "Mother's Day" happens at a different time of the year in North America (May) than it does in Norway (Feb), Afghanistan (March), and Thailand (August), for example.

Why is it Important to Understand This?

Many of the merchandisers' decisions are based on the curation of books they feel are relevant for the readers in the territory that they live in or oversee. Their job includes looking at thousands of titles and making split-second decisions on whether or not to include a book in their merchandising plans based on historical information about known authors, publishers and series titles as well as the following elements:

- **Cover**: Professional, relevant for target audience/genre
- **Metadata**: Title/Author/Series Info/Book Description - clear for target audience / professional sales copy with no errors/typos
- **Price**: Reasonable for target audience.

If the merchandiser for Australia sees that your price isn't optimised for the Australian dollar, they will likely pass on it without giving it a second thought.

A Tale of Two Price Points

To get your book into most of the high visibility spots in the Kobo store, you need to catch a merchandiser's eye. The following example is perhaps an exaggeration, but it illustrates how a Kobo merchandiser might decide on which titles they feature on the main page.

Let's suppose that a merchandiser has two great books they are considering for a single spot. Both are relevant for the feature spot, and both have a great cover, synopsis, and overall look that would fit nicely in that slot. The only difference between the two is that one book is listed at $0.99 and the other one is $9.99.

Which title is that merchandiser most likely to select?

Merchandisers have targets to hit, which are usually based on revenue rather than on unit sales. With that in mind, let's consider the question again.

Which of the two books are they most likely to choose?

Let's look at the math.

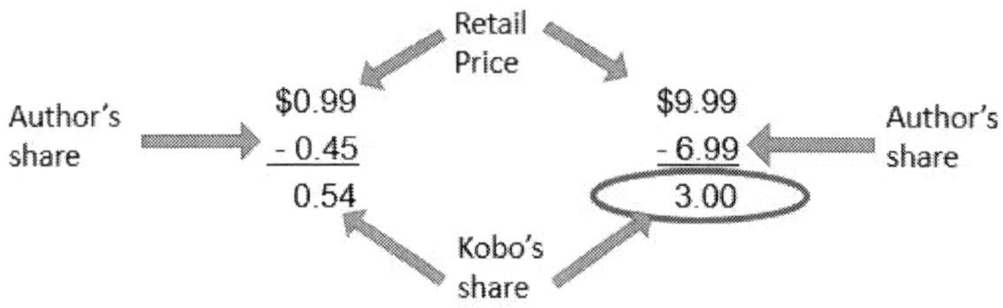

The book priced at $0.99 will earn the author $0.45 per unit sale. That leaves $0.54 for Kobo.

The $9.99 book will earn the author $6.99 which leaves $3.00 for Kobo.

Yes, there are other factors at play, here. The $0.99 cent book would have to sell 5 or more copies in order to earn more than the $9.99 one.

But, as we have already covered, Kobo customers aren't as price sensitive and haven't been conditioned (like they regularly are at Amazon) to only be sniffing out the "discount" and "bargain" bins.

At Kobo, it's very likely that the featured book would sell almost as many copies at the higher price point than it would at the lower one.

And Kobo merchandisers know this.

And they want to keep their jobs.

Let us again wager on which price point is most likely to win that coveted spot.

By way of a conclusion, to stand the best chance of being a featured title, your book needs to have:

- A great, professional cover that works in the territory for the specific genre/category
- Metadata (synopsis, etcetera) that speaks to that same target audience (and the merchandiser who is considering that audience)
- A price that is optimized for the region and gives the merchandiser the best chance of hitting their sales targets

While understanding this is valuable in general, you aren't entirely on your own in terms of trying to get merchandising support.

The good news is that the Kobo Writing Life team has a person responsible for pitching KWL authored titles to the merchandisers as well as curating titles for selected monthly features. In the next chapter, ***The Kobo Writing Life Promotions Tool,*** we'll look at this process and how promotions via KWL work.

Kobo's "Tell Us About Your New Releases"

While there is never any guarantee that your book will be included in a "new releases" feature, you can be sure that if nobody at Kobo knows about it, it definitely WON'T be featured.

So, if you have a book up at Kobo that is in pre-order and the release date is two or more months in the future, you might try to fill out their online "Tell Us About Your New Releases" form.

You can find the form here:

http://bit.ly/KoboNewRelease

As mentioned, there's no guarantee that the book will be featured. But it never hurts for a merchandiser to have looked at a title.

Perhaps they see a title here prior to the book's release but don't do anything with it because it's a day they looked at a thousand other titles and it got passed over. But then they see it again when you submit it for a promotion once the book is live. Perhaps that tiny bit of familiarity is all it takes for them to feel a bit more warmly towards your book.

And perhaps that makes a small difference, but enough of a difference, to get accepted in the promo.

No guarantee. There never is.

But you never can tell.

THE KOBO WRITING LIFE PROMOTIONS TOOL

ONE OF THE MOST valuable assets inside the Kobo Writing Life publishing platform is the PROMOTIONS tab. This is a tool that was designed specifically to help you get your eBook greater visibility in the Kobo store. It provides you with an easy and systematic way to submit your titles into a consideration process for the people on the Kobo Writing Life team who help push KWL authored titles to merchandisers.

Is this chapter we will walk through the tool itself, how it works, and look at the promotions that have typically served most authors in the most positive fashion.

What is the KWL PROMOTIONS Tool?

The KWL Promotions tool is a tab that (as of the

summer and early Fall of 2018) is not automatically available to all KWL users.

It was created as a way for authors to submit their titles for consideration for various curated promotional spots. The people on the KWL team continue to cham-pion these spots for indie authors in order to get KWL-published titles greater exposure and increase sales.

It is important to remember that the KWL team benefits when an author's sales increase (since Kobo only makes money when a book sells) and that their underlying desire is that all KWL authors find success through new readers and increased sales volume at Kobo.

That is why the cost structure (as we will look at) is one that works mostly in favor of an author's interests.

How do you get access to the KWL Promo Tab?

The PROMOTIONS tab appears in the main header of the KWL dashboard. If your KWL account has access to it, you will see it between eBOOKS and AUTHOR SERVICES.

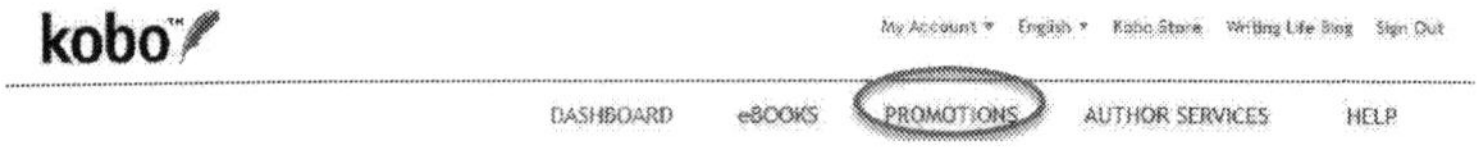

If you don't see it, email *writinglife@kobo.com* and ask the team for access. Remember, there are humans on the other end, so it never hurts to add a little something interesting, unique and friendly to your request to make a good impression.

How do KWL Promotions Work?

Upcoming promotions will appear in this tab as the KWL team negotiates for space for KWL titles in various Kobo promotions.

Given that the Kobo merchandisers typically are planning out promotions 6 to 12 weeks ahead, the promotions you'll see here will most likely be ones that are available in the next 3 to 12 weeks.

Sometimes, in the case of promotions that either haven't already been filled, or in which the final decision isn't made until after the submission period, promotions might still be open until the very last day of submissions.

As of the writing of this chapter, there is no automated or systematic way to be informed of new promotions that are added, so I would recommend logging in at least once a week (perhaps scheduling this task late on a Monday afternoon, for example) and looking for new promotions.

If you follow the Facebook group *The International Indie Author* the groups administrator, Mark Williams has been in the habit of sharing the newly added promotions to that group.

http://bit.ly/InternationalIndieAuthor

Here is an example of a promotion, with the various elements broken down.

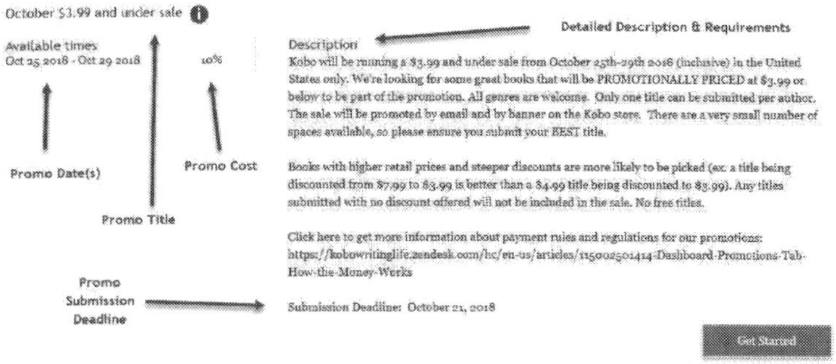

In the example above, you can see what the promotion is called, a detailed description that outline the requirements, what territory the promotion is running in, the cost of the promotion, when it will be running, and the submission deadline.

Here is where you can also quickly preview the eligibility rules if you hover over the little "i" in the red circle that appears to the right of the Promotion title.

As you browse through the available promotions, once you find a promotion that you believe is suitable for one of the titles in your author library, select the GET STARTED button, where you'll see even more details about the terms and costs under *Eligibility rules*.

Eligibility rules

- The eBook must be available in United States.
- Your eBook must be priced between $0.99 and $3.99 USD.
- The eBook must be categorized as Fiction & Literature, Kids & Teens, Mystery & Suspense, Romance, or Sci Fi & Fantasy

On the screen that opens once you click on the GET STARTED button is where you select your title and also where you confirm, enter or update the pricing for that title for the promotional period and also agree to the terms.

What are the Terms?

As of the summer of 2018, here are the basic terms for KWL Promotions:

- Kobo has the right to grant access to the promotion tool at their sole discretion.
- Kobo has the right to reject any Work.
- Authors may choose to submit their Works for promotional consideration using the promotion tool via the KWL dashboard. The terms of each promotion vary by the type of promotion selected, and the submission guidelines and eligibility criteria for each promotion are set out in the KWL dashboard.
- By agreeing to submit their Work for inclusion in any given promotion, the author agrees to the terms of that promotion as set out in the KWL dashboard.
- Kobo reserves the right to change or cancel any promotion. In such instances Kobo will do their best to provide advance notice, as well as another equal opportunity at a different time. In submitting a Work for a promotion, the author agrees that Kobo has sole discretion with respect to the execution and scope of the promotion.

What do KWL Promotions Cost?

Because of the high demand for promotional space, most of the promotions posted will have some sort of cost involved.

There are two basic types of costs:

- Flat fee
- A Percentage of Margin

The good news for authors is that most of the KWL promotions don't cost anything up-front and involve a modification to the percentage of margin received for each unit sale.

For example, if you see a % listed (like the 10% in the example above), you don't even need to exchange money. If you get into the promotion, the system will automatically subtract 10% from your earned royalties for each item sold during that promo period. (Meaning you'll get 60% instead of 70% for those sales)

The benefit to this type of promo is that you're never out of pocket; you merely earn slightly less for those extra sales.

The potential downside, particularly if the promotion is hugely successful, is that if the volume of sales is significant, the cost increases.

But, again, on the plus-side, it is one of those "more affordable" options, since you aren't paying anything and are thus not "out of pocket" to be in the promotion.

The promotions based on flat fees range anywhere from $5 to $100.

Those ones you do have to pay for up front, and this payment process is usually in place either because the promotional space is so limited and highly sought after (such as the *Daily Deal* spot) – this is where "prime real estate principles are involved – or for promoting a free title. Because we all know that taking 10% margin off a title priced at $0.00 equals 0.

Which KWL Promotions Work Best?

The KWL team is always experimenting and trying different promotional spots and angles to appeal to their customers. They are working with the main merchandising team to secure spots for KWL authors inside various monthly promos and they also have their own controlled spaces for promotions.

The following are the promotions that, historically, have always offered the best return on investment for authors:

- **Customer Discount Promotions**. These are usually monthly 30% off or 40% off promotions. These don't require you to change your price (Kobo offers customers a coupon code). This means that you don't need to worry about Amazon Kindle doing automatic price-matching., which is an important factor to remember.

Because the customer will be paying a discount off the retail price, you will, of course, be earning less for each book that sells as part of this promo. But usually the higher visibility and higher volume of sales result in a decent windfall for authors.

These promotions either usually cost an additional 10% but sometimes (such as in the example screen shot below for an October promotion), there is no cost to the author (other than the reduction in price for the customer).

- **Free Page listings**. As discussed in the chapter ***The Power of Free,*** this is great for advertising a free lead-gen or "first in series" free title to help generate sales of your other books.

One of the most searched-for terms on Kobo is "free" and the customer care team regularly point Kobo customers to the Free landing page controlled by the KWL team.

- **Editor's Pick Free Spotlight**. This costs more than a generic free page listing but gives your title a feature spot that appears above the carousel of 6 titles, greater visibility and an extra week of promotional listing.

As you can see in the example below, the cost for this spot is significantly higher; and this is because the author who is spending that money is most likely going to see a solid return on that investment in their sell-through of their other titles.

Free Page - Editor's Pick - Romance

Available times
Oct 22 2018 - Oct 28 2018 $50.00 CAD

- **Buy More Save More** (BMSM). While a bit less common, these promos can be effective, because of the way that the Kobo store promotes the titles. There is not only usually a landing page and a header banner pointing to the sale, but the item page for each book in the promotion usually links back to the sale, and, any time a customer drops a BMSM title into their shopping cart, there is a pop-up notification that they have a chance to save if they purchase more titles from that BMSM campaign.

Meaning that if a customer buys any of the often hundreds of titles in such a promo, there's a chance they'll be prompted to visit an item page where they might also add your book to their shopping cart.

Here's how the math for these types of promotions work.

For example, for a typical sale, which might be a Buy 2 Get 1 Free promotion (3 books for the price of 2), when a customer buys 3 books in this sale, the cheapest title is discounted by 100%.

The cost of that 100% is amortized across all three titles in that customer's shopping cart (so that, while that one book is "free" from the customer's point of view), the cost to the publisher or author is spread across all three titles.

During the month following the promotion you will receive your monthly sales report from Kobo, and those titles that were purchased during the sale will have a reduced royalty rate reflective of the discount that is divided amongst all eBooks purchased at one time. In this case, because the offer is Buy 2 get 1 Free, each eBook purchased will have their royalty reduced by 33% of that total discounted value.

What About Rejection?

If you get rejected for a KWL promotion, don't despair. Like other promotional platforms (such as BookBub, eReader News Today or Bargainbooksy) there are often hundreds of titles submitted for every single promo spot.

Also, if you get rejected from a promo, go to the PROMOTIONS tab and take a look at the status detail (which is something the merchandiser selects from a drop-down list when rejecting titles) and check to see if there are further details provided. The further details are manually human-entered tips that might assist you by helping you understand why your title was rejected.

Here are a few examples of different promotional reasons.

In the example below, the title was rejected because the price isn't in line with the expected/preferred "localized" prices of either .99 or .49 in the territory the promo is running.

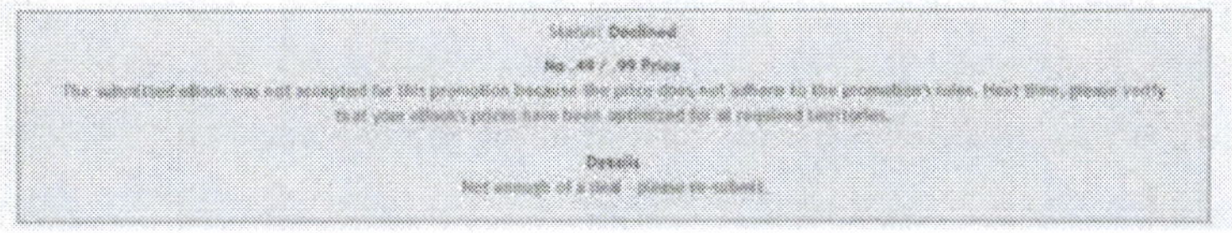

In this next example, the book that was submitted wasn't in the proper category. You not only see the reason code, but you also see a manually entered note from the merchandiser informing the author to re-submit it under a specific category.

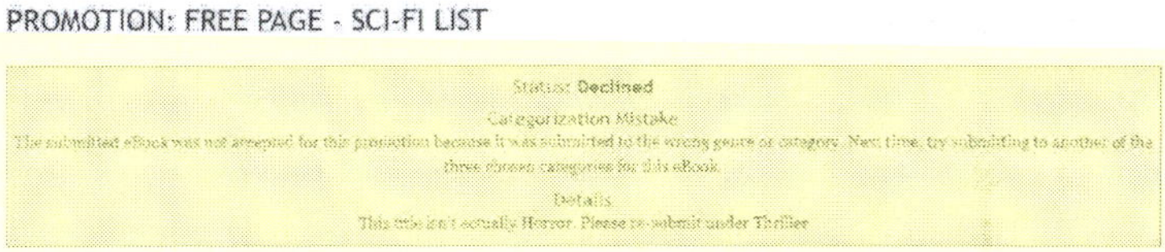

Do keep in mind that, most of the time, there are so many submissions that your title might not even be looked at. Imagine that 1000 titles were submitted to a promo that only required 100 books. If the merchandiser found 100 great titles by the time they got halfway through looking at submissions and your book was somewhere in the list beyond those first 500 titles, your book might have been bulk rejected without anyone looking at it.

It's important to remember, this wasn't a personal rejection of you or of your book.

So, submit again.

And again.

Just be careful to not submit to every single promotion and that you take the time to carefully read the requirements for each to ensure your title and price fits in with the expected results.

And, if you continue to submit a title and it continues to get rejected, but it comes back with no particular reason code, you can either assume that it was just "too far back in the line" to be seen, or you can also consider emailing the KWL team to politely ask for their opinion on the title so that you can, in the future, make more strategic submission decisions.

Again, don't be rude. Just remember there are humans on the other end making decisions that they feel is best for their business; and they can often be overwhelmed with more titles than they can look at. However, taking the time to ask them for their professional opinion (so long as you're not doing it too often), shows your willingness to grow and learn as a professional author.

Sharing Isn't Just Caring, It's More Earning

Something that many authors fail to do is sharing a promotion that they are a part of.

It might seem obvious, but it happens all the time. Authors submit to a promotion and then sit back and wait for the promo to work all on its own.

When you are part of a promotion, share it.

Share links to the promotion landing page, share a link directly to your book on Kobo (there's information about how to do that in the best way in the ***Other Details & Hacks*** chapter) via social media, and let your email newsletter fans know about the promotion.

Yes, Kobo will send emails to their customers and feature the promotions on part of their web site. But it never hurts (and can only help), if you also let people know about the sale or promotion.

One of the factors that the KWL team considers when selecting books for a promo is whether or not the title is likely to sell. They **want** your book to be successful. They **want** your book to sell. Because that is how they make their money. If the promo goes well, your sales increase and often that little boost is what it takes to feed the algorithms and help your ongoing sales hit that next higher plateau.

Also, if the KWL team sees that you are being positive and actively promoting the sale and your books on Kobo, they are more likely to want to include your books in the next promo.

That old saying "God helps those who help themselves" can be re-adapted here to "the KWL team helps authors who help themselves."

Consider this:

Author A submits a title to a promo, gets accepted for it and then sits back and does nothing.

Author B submits a title to a promo, gets accepted, and then shares the promo, acknowledges any increase in sales and publicly thanks Kobo or the KWL team for the opportunity.

When the next promo comes around, assuming the titles are equal in terms of attractiveness and fit for that promo, if there's only one spot and the merchandiser must decide, which author's title makes it in, which author's book do you think they would be more likely to feature?

In the following chapter we'll look at some of the other selling opportunities through Kobo Writing Life that you might not be familiar with.

My hope is that, on your own writing and publishing path, you take the time to consider your relation and your position with respect to each of those elements, and how you might be able to re-adapt and prescribe them into your own plans for a most successful author journey.

ADDITIONAL REVENUE OPPORTUNITIES VIA KOBO

EARNING MONEY FROM direct sales to customers is great, but Kobo also has additional opportunities to earn revenue that aren't dependent upon traditional retail sales. Is this chapter, we'll look at what those revenue opportunities are and how you can leverage them to earn more.

Library Sales via OverDrive

OverDrive (founded and based in Cleveland, OH) is one of the world's largest digital distributors of eBooks, audiobooks, and other digital assets to libraries and schools. They deliver content to more than 27,000 locations worldwide.

Like Kobo, OverDrive is owned by Rakuten (the official company name is Rakuten OverDrive, Inc) and the two sister companies share similar goals in focusing on reading.

When I attended one of the bi-annual conferences for librarians that OverDrive hosts in the summer 2017 I was inspired and moved by the depth and passion for books and for reading that is at the core of the company, as evidenced through the opening remarks to the conference from OverDrive President and CEO Steve Potash.

Like Michael Tamblyn, Kobo CEO, Steve Potash's passion for reading and for enabling others to read freely is in the very lifeblood of the company.

In a 2018 editorial on the *Perspectives on Reading* website, Potash wrote the following in an article entitled *Supporting those on the frontlines attacking illiteracy*:

> *"Our libraries offer a beacon of hope against the rising tide of low literacy skills. For families struggling to survive below the poverty limit, libraries provide free resources for all ages, including story time and reading programs for children. Many also offer tutoring and literacy classes for adults. For individuals who speak and read a native language other than English, libraries offer language learning classes. Parents working non-traditional hours know that the library is a safe space for their children to spend time after school.*

"The value that libraries contribute to their communities cannot be understated. Time and time again, across multiple states and countries, study after study shows that for every $1 in library funding, there's a $4-$5 economic benefit to the community. Supporting our local libraries is the most effective and efficient way to address the literacy crisis head on.

"Reading, and having the ability to read, allows our neighbors and friends to make informed decisions regarding their mental and physical health. Literacy provides opportunities for jobs and career advancement. Literacy offers a secure and safe environment for children to grow and thrive. Acquiring literacy skills as an adult can alter the course of an individual's life, putting them on a path toward personal and professional success. With improved literacy comes improved job opportunities. Gainful employment allows families to flourish, giving children the opportunity to break the poverty cycle created by illiteracy."

Potash and his wife Loree are at the heart of *Believe in Reading* (www.believeinreading.org), created to fund programs dedicated to teaching and encouraging reading for all ages anywhere in the world.

The parallels between Kobo and OverDrive are, indeed, more than just on the surface. They run deep.

So, too, do the systematic connections that you can leverage to reach even more readers and increase your revenue.

Kobo Writing Life has an easy-to-use OPT-in option that allows you to get your eBook distributed into OverDrive's catalog that libraries purchase from.

How to Opt-in Your eBook to the OverDrive Catalog

It's relatively simple to get your eBook distributed to OverDrive's library market. Within Kobo Writing Life, when editing your eBook, go to the ***Rights and Distribution*** tab, scroll down to where you see the *Make Available to Libraries*? Option and click the check-box.

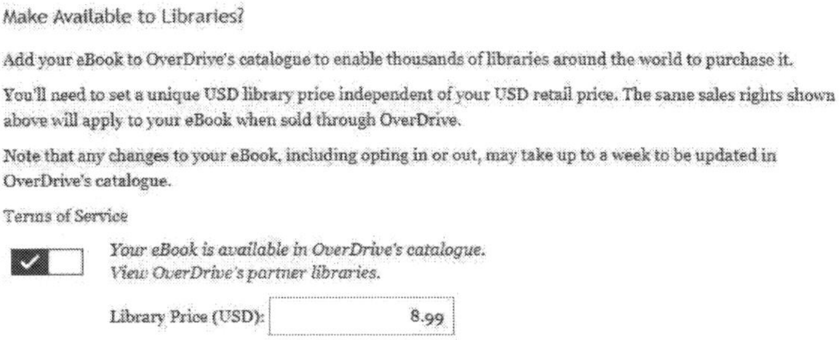

You will need to enter a USD Library Price (which is separate from your regular USD Retail Price). The recommended USD library price (based on standard practice) is that the library price should be between 1.5 and 3 times the regular price of the book.

The library price is reflective of a library purchasing a single copy that they can loan to their customers 1 borrow at a time. Thus, the price is a bit higher to reflect the single income opportunity for multiple reads.

In the screen shot example above, I used the $8.99 USD library price for this book, which is priced at $4.99 USD. I decided to go with 2X, which is right in the middle of the recommended range.

If charging $6.99 to $8.99 USD to the library market for a $4.99 USD retail title seems steep, just consider the fact that most of the "Big Five" published titles following the same library pricing model are charging libraries between $20 and $40 USD.

When I was at Kobo and I was speaking to librarians about KWL authored titles, I would point out an author such as Diane Capri, who writes authorized "Jack Reacher" tales in her "The Hunt for Reacher" series about FBI agents on the trail of Lee Child's most popular character. For the price of a single Lee Child novel, the library could easily purchase two or three of Capri's books and satisfy many of the hundreds of patrons typically on the waiting list for the latest Reacher adventure.

And, because it's important to remember this, the library price (which is only in USD) is completely independent of the retail price. So, you can modify either the retail price (for a temporary sales promotion), or the library price (for a library promotion) but don't have to change them at the same time.

If you are not publishing to Kobo directly, you might still have the option of opting in to the OverDrive system. Draft2Digital, for example, allows the same feature of opting in and setting a unique library price. Smashwords also has this feature.

How Library Sales Reporting Works

For every library sale through Kobo Writing Life, you'll earn 50% of the USD Library Price. Sales are (as of the summer of 2018) not reported in your online dashboard but appear in the separate sales report excel spreadsheet available to you following a month where you have any sales.

(Spreadsheets are not created if no sales happened in that period).

The library purchase details appear as additional information in the title field of your sales spreadsheet (see below for an example).

Title	List Price	Tax Exclude	COGS %
Eden's Eyes	3.9900	3.99	0.7
Finders Keepers	3.9900	3.47	0.7
Sean Costello Thriller Box Set	10.9900	10.99	0.7
Last Call	0.9900	0.99	0.45
Last Call	0.9900	0.99	0.45
Eden's Eyes (Overdrive: Pikes Peak Library District (CO))	4.9900	4.99	0.5
Terminal House (Overdrive: Greater Sudbury Public Library (CA))	6.9900	6.99	0.5
Last Call (Overdrive: Pikes Peak Library District (CO))	6.9900	6.99	0.5
Last Call (Overdrive: Las Vegas-Clark County Library District (NV))	4.9900	4.99	0.5
Here After (Overdrive: Las Vegas-Clark County Library District (NV	4.9900	4.99	0.5
Eden's Eyes (Overdrive: Essex County Library (CA))	4.9900	4.99	0.5
Terminal House (Overdrive: Greater Sudbury Public Library (CA))	6.9900	6.99	0.5
Here After (Overdrive: Pikes Peak Library District (CO))	6.9900	6.99	0.5

As you can see in the sample spreadsheet, Sean Costello's title *Last Call* sold both through the retail channel during a special price drop on the regular retail price to $0.99 (lines 5 and 6), but it also sold, through OverDrive, to two different libraries in Colorado and Nevada. His novel *Eden's Eyes* also has a regular retail sale as well as library sales in Colorado and California. And *Terminal*

House was bought more than once in Sudbury, Ontario (the "CA" in that case is for Canada and not California).

Kobo Plus Subscription Reading Services

With their partner BOL in the Netherlands and Belgium, Kobo offers an "all you can read" subscription service called *Kobo Plus*. KWL authors can opt their titles into this platform and earn money from reads from those customers.

This is currently only available in NL and BE.

The Netherlands is a huge reading market not just for Dutch language titles, but also for English language books; and BOL is a major retailer in that market, giving Kobo a strong presence.

Kobo Plus, of course, provides an even larger opportunity for discoverability and earnings.

As my ex-boss Pieter Swinkels, *Executive Vice President, Rakuten Kobo* and former publisher from the Netherlands says, "Kobo Plus allows readers to effortlessly discover new authors and try new genres that they might not otherwise try, encouraging people to read more."

It is also important to note two unique features about the *Kobo Plus* program.

- Unlike Amazon's *Kindle Unlimited* subscription program (which independent authors can only get into if they are in the KDP Select exclusivity program), you are not required to have the title exclusive to Kobo to participate.

- In addition, having your title listed in *Kobo Plus* means that your title will be listed in 2 additional browse catalogs for Kobo and BOL consumers in NL and BE. (IE, a single eBook will be listed in 4 places rather than the regular 2 places, which increases your discoverability in those markets)

How to Opt into Kobo Plus

On the ***Rights and Distribution*** tab for your eBook in Kobo Writing Life, click on the check box to opt your title into Kobo Plus. There is no need to enter or modify your pricing information.

And, just to be 100% clear, there is no need to be exclusive to Kobo. You can be in the *Kobo Plus* program and still be published wide to any and all retail channels around the globe.

Do note that if you opt a title in to the *Kobo Plus* program, you cannot opt that title out for a 3-month period. **This is not the same as exclusivity.** The reason this requirement exists is that it takes time and resources inside Kobo and inside BOL to plan for merchandising as well as finding new markets. Remember, as we discussed in the chapter about Kobo merchandisers, they often plan things out 6 to 12 weeks in advance. So having titles appear and disappear from a section of the catalog creates planning issues. That is why this 3-month window exists.

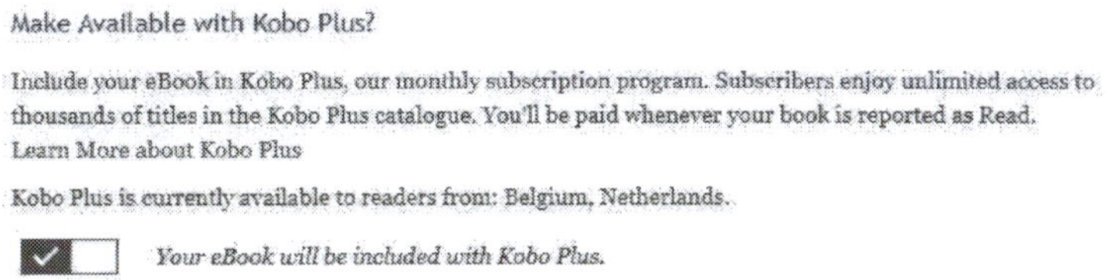

If you aren't published to Kobo through Kobo Writing Life you can still opt into *Kobo Plus* through such third-party distributors as Draft2Digital.

How Kobo Plus Reading Data Earnings Reporting Works

You earn revenue for any Kobo Plus read of 20% or more of your eBook. The money earned is based on a calculation (see further reading) of a number of factors based on a shared revenue tally.

Reading data and earnings do not appear in the online dashboard and come, monthly, in a separately reported spreadsheet that you can download from your KWL dashboard.

The spreadsheet has a slightly different naming convention than the regular sales spreadsheet. For example, my June 2018 sales spreadsheets from Kobo Writing Life have the following names:

- sales_invoice_PUB_2018_06
- sales_invoice_SUBS_2018_06

The one with "SUBS" in the file name is my *Kobo Plus* earnings report.

The details of the read and the payment, re-calculated back from EUR to your default currency, will look like the example below (from my June 2018 report).

Read date	Publisher name	eISBN	Author	Title	List price	List price (TaxCu	List p	Region	Read threshold (%	Reads	Total payable	Foreign	Total in payable c
2018-06-28	Stark Publishing	9780973568837	Brit Trog	Campus Chills	4.49	3.71	EUR	NL	0.2	1	0.98	1.4556	1.42
2018-06-07	Stark Publishing	1230002354170	Mark Les	Dark Shadows	2.99	2.47	EUR	NL	0.2	1	0.65	1.4556	0.94

As you can see, I earned $2.36 from two titles in NL in June.

That income is certainly not life-changing, but it is an additional few dollars earned in a territory where I normally don't get all that many sales. And I've earned most of my writing income through gradual and incremental increases over time.

So I'll happily take it.

I have also noticed a slight increase in my sales into NL since opting all my titles into the *Kobo Plus* program and I know, having spoken to hundreds of authors, that many authors are doing quite well and earning a respectable amount of money on their English language titles in NL and BE via the *Kobo Plus* program.

Affiliate Opportunity

Affiliate income can be an important part of an author's income, particularly when you look at the effect of incremental revenue sources over time.

The Kobo affiliate program is operated through Kobo's sister company Rakuten Affiliate Network (formerly known as LinkShare)

The program allows you to earn 5% commission on eBooks and 10% commission on devices and accessories. Kobo Writing Life authors also get a 1% bonus of additional commission for their eBook sales through this program.

The system is not as easy to use nor as intuitive as the Amazon program, but again, it's an additional opportunity for increasing your revenue earnings.

There are articles about the program on the Kobo Writing Life blog at www.kobowritinglife.com, but you can also email kobo-affiliates@rakuten.com for more details and how to sign up.

Audiobooks

Audiobooks at Kobo, launched the summer of 2017, represents a new and exciting opportunity for authors as the growth of audiobooks is predicted to see the same massive waves that eBooks had just a few years ago.

The Kobo app for iOS and Android includes the ability to read eBooks or listen to audiobooks; and the Kobo store cross-merchandises eBooks and audiobooks, making them easily accessible to all customers.

As of this writing, I know that the KWL team is working at allowing authors to import their audiobook titles directly through the KWL dashboard (the release of that functionality is not yet known); but currently, the best ways to get your audiobooks to Kobo's catalog would be if the audiobook is available through a major publisher or distributor, or via an audio-book specialist such as ListenUp Audio (available link through KWL's *Author Services*), or via Findaway Voices.

Findaway Voices partnered with Draft2Digital in 2017 to allow self-published authors access to affordable professional audio-creation services as well as the ability to upload audiobooks already produced, while maintaining control of the retail price. Findaway Voices is currently the best way for an independent author to get their eBook into Kobo's catalog.

If you have a title published through Draft2Digital, even if that title isn't published to Kobo via D2D, you can click a button and have the metadata ported over to a Findaway Voices account for simplicity in starting the audiobook setup. Not only that but coming in through Draft2Digital saves you the $49 USD setup fee for using the Findaway Voices production resources.

OTHER DETAILS & HACKS

AS I WAS compiling the content for this book, I kept coming across little things that I wasn't sure where to add in. Some of the elements felt like they might deserve their own chapter, while others just floated around as part of a "get to this" list.

By the time I got to the end of the first draft I realized that those little pieces that didn't seem to have a home could be inserted into a single chapter of miscellaneous tidbits.

And that's exactly what you have here.

Author Services

Because they know the importance of having a professional editor and cover design as well as other professional and promotional services, the Kobo Writing Life team continues to work with trusted third-party service providers to find tools, services and platforms that authors are likely to find valuable.

In most cases, the service comes with a special coupon code or discount that KWL authors can use to save money on the services.

Examples of such services (as of the summer of 2018), include:

- 10% off a Custom-Designed Cover at Damonza
- Custom Book Cover Design from AcePub
- A discount ($25 USD off) the purchase of an ISBN for US-based authors (via Bowker)
- A discount of $100 USD off the hourly rate for audiobook creation via ListenUp Audio
- The creation of a professional ePub
- $20 USD off a chance to get a Publishers Weekly Select review
- A copyright service via Digi-Rights for assistance with managing copyright

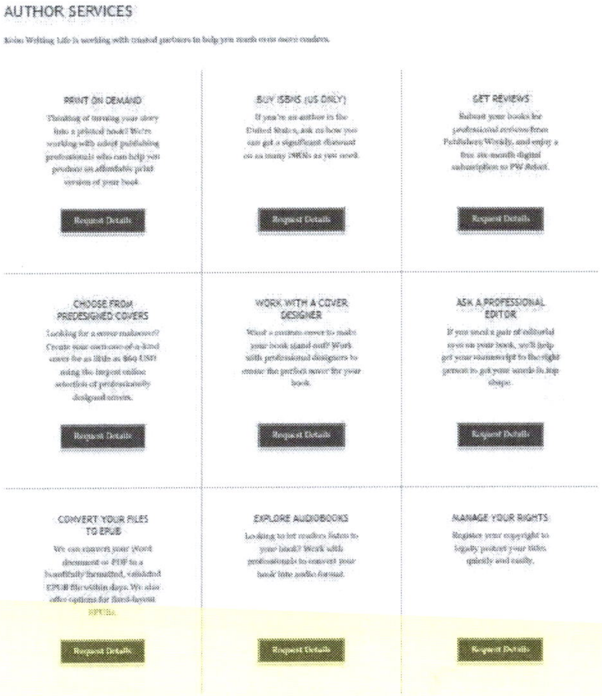

Notification Bar

When there is something to notify authors about (most likely a new feature, an update to terms of service or perhaps a maintenance window where the KWL system might be temporarily down), you might see a message appearing immediately below the main header view on your KWL dashboard.

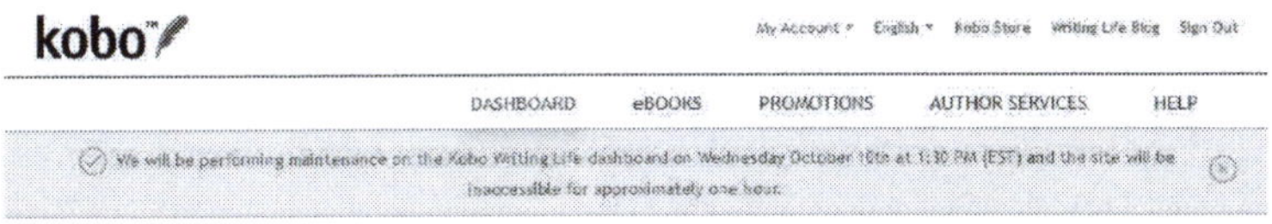

Regardless of the specific message or type of notification, they will come in one of two manners.

Dismissible or non-dismissible.

If, like in the example above, the notification is dismissible, you can click the little X symbol inside the circle to dismiss and remove it from cluttering up your view.

When the notification is not-dismissible, there won't be a little X inside a circle and the message will likely be highlighted in a different color (usually red). This is usually due to the message being considered important by the KWL team.

The Kobo Writing Life Help Centre

As of the summer of 2017, the KWL team maintains an ongoing and regularly updated help centre via the Zendesk controlled page:

http://bit.ly/KWLZendesk

This easy to navigate and often interactive page is a great resources for authors to learn more, to connect directly with the KWL team as well as to engage with others from the KWL community.

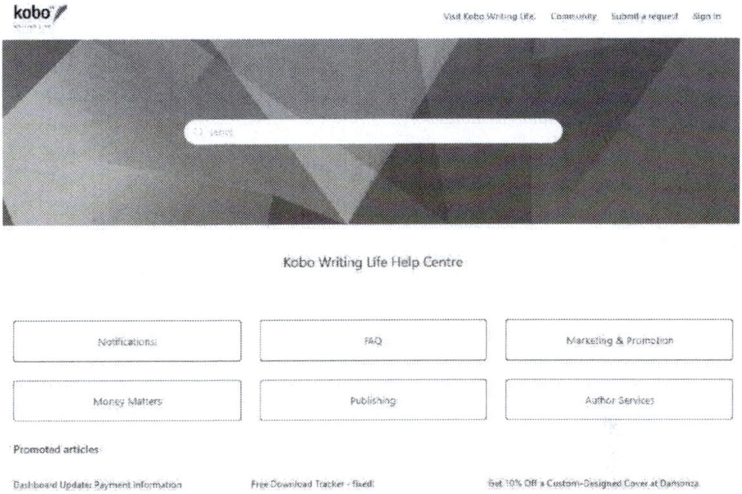

It is something I recommend you check out, particularly if you have any questions that you want answers for on your own, or via posting a question and having someone from the KWL team, or the KWL community respond.

Localization and Linking to Books on Kobo

Because Kobo is a global store and the URL you end up landing on will most likely be auto-re-directed to your own local country and language, here's a handy shortcut for linking to your books on Kobo in a more universal way.

If I were to go look at the URL for one of my books at Kobo, the title *Evasion* for example, I would see:

https://www.kobo.com/ca/en/ebook/evasion

In the URL, the kobo.com is followed by /ca/en which are the country and language indicators. In this case, they are referring to "Canada" and "English."

If you are in the US, when you search for and find the book, you would see:

https://www.kobo.com/us/en/ebook/evasion

Notice the "us" instead of "ca" to indicate the United States. If, you are in the US, and you click on the Canadian link above, you would see, instead of a "BUY" button, a box that would direct you to click a US flag icon to shop for the book via the United States.

The best way to share a link to your book so that it automatically re-directs your customer to their own local territory is to strip out the /us/en or the /ca/en and just use the core basic link. Like this:

https://www.kobo.com/ebook/evasion

If you click on that link and you are in Canada, it'll take you to the /ca/en landing page. If you're in the US, you'll be re-directed to the US equivalent.

You might also use the following convention by using the ISBN for the book.

https://www.kobo.com/Search?Query=9780973568868

The link above will take you to my book *A Canadian Werewolf in New York.*

Here's another note on the naming convention for a book. By default, the title of the book is adapted into the URL.

My book *One Hand Screaming* is adapted into:

https://www.kobo.com/ebook/one-hand-screaming

Notice the dashes between words in the title:

My novel *A Canadian Werewolf in New York* for example, uses the same format.

https://www.kobo.com/ebook/a-canadian-werewolf-in-new-york

But now take a look at my eBook *Night Cries*:

https://www.kobo.com/ebook/night-cries-4

You'll notice that it has a "-4" at the end of the title. That is because there are 3 other books with that same title that were published to Kobo's catalog before my book with that same title.

If you go to the URL and change the 4 to a 3, you'll find a different book.

Sometimes, if the earlier published book is no longer active, you might get a 404 error.

But at least that's how you'll understand why some URLs are titles, while others have the extra numbers tacked on to the end of them.

Finding your Dummy ISBN

You aren't required to use an ISBN when you publish your eBook to Kobo. If you don't enter one, the Kobo system will assign your book a "Dummy" ISBN in order to track it.

This "Dummy" ISBN is used for internal tracking purposes and is not a real ISBN.

The Dummy ISBNs start with the numbers 1234.

In the early days of Kobo Writing Life, the next 9 digits were merely sequential. It wasn't until a few years after thousands of titles were published that the protocol was updated to ensure that the dummy ISBNs followed the standard EAN-13 check-digit format. This was adapted into the system because some of Kobo's newer retail partners wouldn't allow a 13-digit UPC/EAN code that didn't pass the check-digit test.

If you ever need to know the dummy ISBN (when emailing the Kobo Writing Life team about a title, for example, does make the process easier if you indicate the ISBN in question), you can find it on your book's item page on Kobo.

Go to your item page. Scroll down to below the Ratings and Reviews section. On the bottom left side of the screen you'll see your publisher name, the publication date, the Imprint (if you entered one), the ISBN, the language and the format/download options, as well as whether or not the book has DRM.

eBook Details

Stark Publishing, July 2013
Imprint: Stark Publishing
ISBN: 1230000149371
Language: English
Download options: EPUB 2 (DRM-Free)

The example above is for my eBook *Spirits*. You can find/copy the ISBN from that location.

Social Promotion

When you have a new book at Kobo, be sure to tell the world about it. Most authors just send out links to their book on Amazon and leave it at that.

While I have long been a huge advocate for using the free Books2Read.com universal book links from Draft2Digital as my main link (since it is inclusive of ALL eBook retail sites via a single convenient link), it never hurts to share a Kobo specific link and tag the folks at Kobo to let them know you're sharing your book with a link to their catalog.

Here are some of the Kobo social media platform accounts:

Twitter
Kobo Writing Life (@KoboWritingLife)
Kobo (@Kobo)
Kobo Deals (@KoboDeals)

Instagram

Kobo Writing Life (@Kobo.Writing.Life)
Kobo (@KoboBooks)

LinkedIn
Kobo Writing Life: https://www.linkedin.com/showcase/kobo-writing-life/
Kobo: https://www.linkedin.com/company/kobo-inc-/

CONCLUSION

I REALLY SHOULD have known I would write this book. In retrospect, it makes complete sense. However, at the beginning, it was merely going to be a slightly longer chapter in my book *Indie Publishing Insider Secrets*.

But, as I was writing the first draft of that book, the chapter on Kobo kept getting longer and longer. As it started to surpass 18,000 words, even before turning the book over to my editor, I realized I was going to have to cut that chapter down significantly.

At about the same time, Reedsy (where I am listed as a marketing/publishing consultant) reached out and asked if I would be willing to write a 10-day free email course on "Kobo Hacks" for them.

Each of the 10 daily emails would be somewhere in the realm of 500 words.

"Excellent," I thought. "An exercise to help me trim and cut."

At 500 words per daily lesson, that would force me to cut all this information for the Kobo chapter down to about 5,000 words

I worked at doing that. Martin at Reedsy was a great editor to work with on that, and as we went back and forth he helped me refine it to a nice core basis.

The course is a great and free quick access option to much of the same information that appears in this book. But there are less examples, and less details.

So, when I went back to the about 5,000 words and attempted a re-write, I kept wanting to expand and explain things in more detail. Before I got through half of the content, I was already back to 8,000 words.

"You know what you need to do," my editor said when we were discussing the progress of my forthcoming book. We had already had a similar discussion on the earlier chapter on the *P's of Publishing Success*, which we decided to roll out into its own smaller book.

"Yeah," I said. "I know. It seems to be a pattern."

"So, what do you want to call it?" they said with a big smirk.

"Something with alliteration." I tossed out ideas that came to mind and *Kracking Kobo* was one of them.

Even though this conversation was over the phone, I could hear their eyes rolling.

"You're killing me," they said.

"Killing you? That's good!"

And so, the title was born from that.

Titles are a funny thing. Although I am an optimist, I am not one to use hyperbole. I get frustrated when I read the promises that various books or services make about how authors can become rich just by following their advice.

But I also had to use an attention-grabbing title.

Not to mention my affinity for alliteration.

Do I believe that, following information and advice in this book, you can *kill it* on Kobo?

Sure.

This isn't to say that you're going to immediately be making six figures a month from Kobo; but I do know there are authors who earn that from Kobo in a year. I know a lot more authors who make a respectable four and five figure income from Kobo, and that, if Kobo is a single retailer among the main four or five big ones for English language titles, that earning four figures a month at Kobo likely means they are bringing in a respectable five figure or six figure income from all retailers combined.

I believe that you can certainly increase your sales and earnings at Kobo by applying a number of different techniques and by treating it like the unique sales platform it is.

And I know that it takes a long time to earn decent revenue from Kobo. It often takes upwards of 6 to 9 months. In some cases, with authors I've known and worked with, it took them more than two years to establish a consistent and comfortable base-line of sales on

Kobo. Much longer than it took them to establish a similar base on Amazon or other retailers.

There are, of course, exceptions. In early 2018 when author T S Paul contacted me to let me know what he was earning on Kobo a mere two months into his "publishing wide" experience, I didn't, at first, believe his sales numbers.

"There's no way you're making that much," I said. "You've only been on Kobo for a couple of months. It normally takes six or more months to ramp up to four figures a month."

But he showed me his sales dashboard.

It can happen. He followed some of my advice, and he also applied his own unique strategy too. That combination seems to be working well from him.

And I know, from other authors, that applying some of the advice in this book with your own strategy that is unique to your books and your readership, it is entirely possible to create an "up-and-to-the-right" sales result on Kobo. Some of it will come from incremental increases where you leverage the opportunities for global sales in new markets and some of it will stem from increased margin and revenue in the existing ones.

So, you can increase your earnings on Kobo.

And perhaps, for most authors who aren't bringing in five and six figure incomes, *killing it* on Kobo is a relative term related to where you are starting.

With perhaps a handful of exceptions, increasing your sales and your revenue via a retailer like Kobo isn't an overnight thing, and it might not, in the short term, be a life-changing event.

But, cumulatively, over time, with enough understanding and hard work, those sales can increase in enough incremental ways to make that difference.

Over time, when you look back at where your sales were and where they are after applying hard work, patience and persistence, you'll realize that you have been *killing it*, even if you might have been killing it softly.

My hope is that the information, insights and reminders that appear in this book are useful and valuable to you on your own writing and publishing path. I sincerely hope that you can adapt them into your own unique writing and publishing journey and apply what works best for you to help you both increase your readership and your overall base income via Kobo's global market.

Now go kill it.

Softly.

Slowly.

Surely.

SELECTED RESOURCES AND FURTHER READING

BELOW YOU WILL find a short list of either some of the resources that I might have referred to throughout the book, or that provide a bit more information on some of the topics discussed.

Many of the articles below come direct from the Kobo Writing Life team at Kobo via www.kobowritinglife.com. You should regularly check this blog out as it is written by the people at Kobo as well as authors who leverage Kobo for their sales.

Online Articles

"Publishing on Kobo: A Step-by-Step Guide"
https://kobowritinglife.com/2017/11/08/publishing-on-kwl-a-step-by-step-guide/

"Who We Are: The People Behind KWL"
https://kobowritinglife.com/who-we-are-the-people-behind-kwl/

"Go Global with Kobo Writing Life"
(A list of the retail partners that Kobo partners with)
https://kobowritinglife.com/2016/11/04/go-global-with-kobo-writing-life/

"Top 5 Reasons Why Books Are Rejected in Publishing on KWL"
https://kobowritinglife.com/2017/08/21/top-5-reasons-books-are-rejected-from-publishing-on-kwl/

"Selling More of Your Series Books on Kobo"
https://kobowritinglife.com/2015/01/29/selling-more-of-your-series-books-on-kobo-11/

"Building Your Global Sales at Kobo"
https://kobowritinglife.com/2016/08/22/build-your-global-sales-with-v-writing-life/

"KWL Guide to Preorders"

https://kobowritinglife.com/2015/07/31/kwl-guide-to-pre-orders/

"How Kendall Ryan Because a Bestselling Kobo Author"
https://kobowritinglife.com/2017/11/01/how-kendall-ryan-became-a-bestselling-kobo-author/

"A Global View on Kobo"
(How to see your books listed in other currencies/other countries)
https://kobowritinglife.com/2017/01/13/a-global-view-on-kobo/

"Using the KWL Price Scheduling Tool"
https://kobowritinglife.com/2013/11/07/kwl-price-scheduling-tool-now-live/

"Author Perspective: How My Sales on Kobo Topped All Other Vendors" (Diana Deverell)
https://kobowritinglife.com/2016/09/09/how-my-sales-on-kobo-topped-all-other-vendors/

"How my $19.99 Box Set Became a #1 Kobo Bestseller" (Lauren Royal)
https://kobowritinglife.com/2015/09/21/how-my-19-99-boxed-set-became-a-1-kobo-bestseller/

"How to Create a Great Box Set"

https://kobowritinglife.com/2016/04/22/how-to-create-a-great-box-set/

"Book Cover Design Tips from a Merchandiser"
https://kobowritinglife.com/2016/05/25/kobo-writing-life-podcast-episode-058-insights-from-kobo-merchandisers/

"How the Money Works" (KWL Dashboard Promotions Tab)
https://kobowritinglife.zendesk.com/hc/en-us/articles/115002501414-Dashboard-Promotions-Tab-How-the-Money-Works

"Distribute to OverDrive via KWL"
https://kobowritinglife.com/2017/11/14/distribute-to-overdrive-via-kwl-hassle-free-library-distribution-50-royalties/

"Why Library Discovery is the Best Discovery"
https://kobowritinglife.com/2018/10/04/why-library-discovery-is-the-best-discovery/

"About Kobo Plus"
https://kobowritinglife.com/contact-us/about/about-kobo-plus/

Podcasts

The Creative Penn

Joanna has a very global view of eBook sales not just for Kobo but for far beyond. Her NRP/CBC/BBC quality podcast interviews are among the best for continuing to learn about future developments in digital publishing.

www.thecreativepenn.com

Stark Reflections on Writing & Publishing

This is my own weekly podcast, started in Jan 2018, where I share interviews as well as my own reflections on things I have learned and am continuing to learn.

www.starkreflections.ca

KWL Podcast Episodes

"Behind the Scenes at Kobo" (KWL Podcast)

https://kobowritinglife.com/2016/04/13/kobo-writing-life-podcast-episode-055-behind-the-scenes-at-kobo/

"Behind the Scenes at Kobo with Sarah Woodbury" (KWL Podcast)

https://kobowritinglife.com/2018/01/17/kobo-writing-life-podcast-episode-100-behind-the-scenes-at-kobo-with-featured-author-sarah-woodbury/

"Insights from Kobo Merchandisers" (KWL Podcast)

https://kobowritinglife.com/2016/05/25/kobo-writing-life-podcast-episode-058-insights-from-kobo-merchandisers/

Websites

The Kobo Writing Life Blog
As mentioned, here's where you can find out information and updates directly from the Kobo Writing Life team.
www.kobowritinglife.com

The Alliance of Independent Authors
A global non-profit association for self-publishing authors and an excellent source for trusted information about Kobo, third party distributors or virtually any digital publishing platform or service.
www.allianceindependentauthors.org

The New Publishing Standard
An e-magazine edited by Mark Williams aimed to help keep writers informed about book publishing news and events that both publishing insiders and newcomers can understand. One of the most global and balanced insights available.
www.thenewpublishingstandard.com

ABOUT THE AUTHOR

Mark's highly successful experience in the publishing and bookselling industry spans more than three decades where he has worked in almost every type of brick and mortar, online and digital bookstore.

The former Director of self-publishing and author relations for Rakuten Kobo, and the founding leader of *Kobo Writing Life*, Kobo's free direct-to-Kobo publishing tool, Mark thrives on innovation, particularly as it relates to digital publishing.

Mark works as Director of Business Development for Draft2Digital and continues to write and mentor and coach authors and publishers about digital publishing opportunities both 1:1 and via his *Stark Reflections on Writing & Publishing* weekly podcast.

You can learn more about Mark at www.markleslie.ca

Selected Books by the Author

Under the name Mark Leslie Lefebvre

Writing & Publishing

The 7 P's of Publishing Success

Killing It on Kobo

Indie Publishing Insider Secrets

Under the name Mark Leslie

Non-Fiction ("Ghost Stories")

Macabre Montreal

Haunted Hospitals

Creepy Capital

Tomes of Terror

Spooky Sudbury

Haunted Hamilton

Fiction

Nocturnal Screams (Short Fiction Series)

A Canadian Werewolf in New York

Evasion

I, Death

Active Reader: And Other Cautionary Tales from the Book World

Bumps in the Night

As Editor

Fiction River: Superstitious

Fiction River: Feel the Love

Fiction River: Feel the Fear

Fiction River: Editor's Choice

Tesseracts Sixteen: Parnassus Unbound

Campus Chills

STARK REFLECTIONS ON WRITING AND PUBLISHING

If you enjoyed this book, you might also like Mark's weekly podcast, ***Stark Reflections on Writing and Publishing***.

Access to publishing has never been easier, and it is an amazing time to be a writer. But it may also be harder than it has ever been. You currently have more choices, more options, more possibilities than ever in the history of publishing.

What paths are right for you on your writing journey?

Drawing upon more than a quarter century of experience as a bookseller, a writer, an editor and a respected and trusted book industry representative, Mark Leslie Lefebvre provides context to help you make informed decisions to build your own writing and publishing life.

Along with interviews with folks from both the traditional publishing and indie-publishing communities, Mark shares his own personal experiences as a writer and industry consultant.

www.starkreflections.ca

27310217R00131

Printed in Great Britain
by Amazon